HIDDEN SIGNS OF THE UNIVERSE

The Secret Code Behind Coincidences, Repetitions, and Synchronicities

Moonlit Feather Books

Everything is speaking. This book will teach you how to listen.

Table of Contents

Part I — Reconnecting with the Signals

We are surrounded by information every moment of our lives. But most of it isn't digital, spoken, or even written. It comes in the form of subtle cues—through experiences, emotions, timing, and patterns that speak not to the intellect, but to something deeper within us. These cues are what we often call "signs." They don't shout. They whisper. And unless we've trained ourselves to listen, we'll walk past them every single day without noticing.

Part I is where we learn to listen again.

Many people go through life unaware of the hidden layers of meaning woven into their daily experiences. They chalk up odd patterns to coincidence, disregard inner tugs as irrational feelings, and overlook small synchronicities as random chance. But what if those moments weren't random at all? What if they were part of a larger language—a personal language—that the universe uses to guide, nudge, or even warn us?

Reconnecting with the signals starts by acknowledging that this language exists. The problem isn't that the universe has stopped speaking to us. The problem is that most of us have forgotten how to hear it.

There's a reason you're drawn to this topic now. Maybe you've experienced patterns you can't explain, or moments that feel too meaningful to be dismissed. Maybe you're tired of ignoring the feeling that there's something more going on—something right beneath the surface. If so, this part of the book will begin to reveal that deeper layer to you.

You'll learn the difference between actual signs and random noise, how to discern their relevance in your life, and what types of signs are most common and most often misunderstood. You'll also begin to understand why so many of us miss these signals for years, even when they're right in front of us.

This is not about superstition or magical thinking. It's about developing awareness. Think of it as tuning your inner radio to a frequency that has always been broadcasting—you just haven't dialed in.

You don't need any special tools or training to begin this reconnection. What you do need is openness, attention, and a willingness to see your life through a slightly different lens. It's a small shift, but it changes everything. Once you start recognizing the signs around you, they appear more frequently, more clearly, and with greater relevance.

This part of the book is foundational. It isn't about dramatic spiritual awakenings or dramatic turning points. It's about gently adjusting your perception so that what was once invisible starts to become undeniable. And with that shift, you'll begin to feel something powerful return—trust. Not in chance or fate, but in your own ability to read the world around you with clarity and intuition.

Let's begin the process of tuning in. Everything that comes later depends on your ability to first reconnect.

Chapter 1: What Spiritual Signs Really Are

The Difference Between Signs, Omens, and Random Events

Not everything that catches your attention is a sign. And not everything strange or unexpected should be taken as a message from the universe. Learning to tell the difference between a true sign, a symbolic omen, and a random event is essential if you want to develop reliable inner guidance. Without that clarity, it's easy to get caught in confusion, reading too much into meaningless patterns or ignoring important signals that could have helped you.

Let's start with signs.

A **sign** is a meaningful cue that resonates with your current state, question, or path. It is not just something strange or unusual—it's something that lands with significance in your experience. Signs are personal. They might appear in the form of symbols, repeated numbers, overheard phrases, sudden interruptions, or anything that grabs your intuitive attention in a way that feels oddly timed or charged. Signs don't always make logical sense, but they hit differently. There's often a quiet sense of "this matters," even if you can't explain why yet.

Signs often feel like guidance. They show up after you've been thinking about something deeply, or when you're stuck between choices. They might come when you've asked for clarity, even without words. And while they can be subtle, their impact is not. Something in you feels gently shaken or confirmed. You can sense that you're being nudged to pause, reflect, or reconsider.

Omens are different.

An **omen** carries weight, but often in a more collective, archetypal, or emotionally charged way. While signs tend to be neutral or personal, omens are often interpreted as forewarnings—good or bad. They're dramatic, layered with myth, and tied to patterns that have cultural or symbolic meaning across time. A black cat crossing your path, a sudden storm, a broken object, or a crow circling above might be seen as omens in certain traditions. But what makes something an omen isn't the event itself. It's how it's interpreted through symbolic history and your inner sense of meaning.

Omens usually stir a visceral reaction. You might feel a wave of discomfort or anticipation. They can be challenging to interpret, because they tend to trigger emotion first and reflection later. The key is to not immediately label something as an omen just because it feels dramatic. Ask yourself: "What does this mean to me?" and "Is this echoing a deeper knowing I've been avoiding?"

Now let's address the third category: random events.

A **random event** is just that—an occurrence without specific relevance to your current path, emotional state, or intuitive process. Not everything odd or unexpected is part of a greater message. The human mind is a pattern-seeking machine, which means it will sometimes try to assign meaning where none exists. That's not a flaw. It's part of how we learn and survive. But it becomes a problem when we give too much weight to something simply because it broke our routine.

The danger of mistaking random events for signs is that it clutters your intuitive channel. You start doubting everything or over-analyzing daily life, trying to extract meaning from every shadow, noise, or delay. That's exhausting. And it's not necessary.

To develop discernment, you need to stay grounded in two things: self-awareness and emotional tone. When a true sign appears, there's usually a sense of clarity or confirmation. When an omen shows up, there's a stirring in your body, an emotional ripple that says "pay attention." And when something is random, it typically fades fast and doesn't stir anything inside of you, no matter how odd it may seem on the surface.

That quiet distinction—between internal resonance and external noise—is the foundation of intuitive mastery. Signs and omens align with your emotional state, your inner questions, or your path of transformation. Random events don't. They lack the deeper echo.

Still, it takes practice to trust this discernment. In the early stages, many people either dismiss everything as coincidence or assume everything is a message. Both extremes block true perception. Dismissing everything flattens your connection to the unseen world, while over-ascribing meaning can lead to paranoia or magical thinking. The goal isn't to swing between skepticism and superstition. It's to cultivate a grounded, intuitive awareness that helps you know when something carries meaning and when it doesn't.

This process becomes easier when you pay attention to emotional texture. Signs often arrive with a sense of invitation. Omens tend to arrive with urgency or caution. Random events feel neutral—sometimes surprising, but quickly forgotten. A meaningful event usually stays with you. It repeats in your mind. You find yourself reflecting on it, sensing that it might contain more than meets the eye.

Your body also helps with discernment. A sign might land as a full-body yes or a subtle opening in your chest. An omen might feel like a tightening, a drop in the stomach, or an instinctive need to pause. A random event doesn't usually evoke any of that—it comes and goes like background noise. When something moves you in a way that makes you feel more awake, more aligned, or more alert, it's worth considering why. That's often the clue.

Context is another piece. A rainbow after a moment of despair might hit differently than a rainbow on a random Tuesday afternoon. The event is the same, but your emotional state, the question in your heart, and the symbolic timing shift everything. Don't separate meaning from context. Without that lens, it's easy to miss personal relevance.

It's also worth recognizing that signs and omens are rarely loud. They often whisper. That's why stillness, reflection, and self-trust matter. You need a quiet inner space to catch the signal. If your mind is racing or filled with external noise, you'll either overlook the signs or misinterpret what you think you see. The more internally clear you are, the more precisely you'll notice when something is out of place—or when something fits too perfectly to be ignored.

Misinterpretation happens when you force meaning. If you're desperate for an answer or afraid of missing guidance, your mind might label everything as a sign. This creates confusion and weakens trust in your intuition. A healthier approach is to hold the event loosely. Ask yourself, "Does this resonate?" and "What does it evoke in me?" Don't rush to answer. Sometimes the meaning unfolds slowly, over hours or even days.

Real signs often integrate themselves into your awareness gently, deepening with time.

Developing discernment also means being willing to be wrong. Not every conclusion you draw will be perfect. That's part of learning. But as long as you stay honest with yourself and refine your attention, your ability to perceive clearly will grow. Over time, you'll start to feel the difference without needing to think about it. Your inner compass will become more accurate, and your relationship with signs, omens, and the flow of life will shift from confusion to quiet confidence.

That's the essence of this work: not to live in fear of missing a message, but to walk through life awake enough to recognize the ones that matter. You are not meant to decode every flicker or coincidence. You are meant to listen deeply, respond truthfully, and trust what calls you forward. The universe doesn't speak in chaos. It speaks in patterns, mirrors, and rhythms that, once felt, cannot be unseen.

How Signs Work Across Cultures and Belief Systems

Wherever humans have existed, they have searched for meaning in the world around them. Long before organized religions or modern psychology, people were already interpreting their environments symbolically. A sudden storm, the flight path of birds, the shape of fire, or a dream before battle—these were never just random events. They were seen as messages from the invisible world. This impulse isn't specific to one region or belief. It's universal.

Every culture has developed its own language of signs. In ancient Egypt, the ibis was associated with wisdom and divine writing. In Norse mythology, ravens were considered messengers of Odin. In Native American traditions, the appearance of certain animals could signify guidance, danger, or spiritual presence. In Eastern philosophies, numbers, directions, and elements held encoded truths about balance and destiny. In all of these systems, the outer world was a mirror of the inner world, and paying attention was a form of spiritual intelligence.

These symbols were rarely abstract. They came from deep connection with the land, the seasons, and the rhythm of life. People didn't just study signs—they lived them. The environment was their teacher. Over time, each culture created its own frameworks to pass on this wisdom. That's how we ended up with dream dictionaries, sacred texts, rituals, and oral traditions that all help decode the hidden messages of life.

But despite the different forms, one truth emerges: the human need to read the world like a message. Whether it's feathers, numbers, animal encounters, or strange coincidences, people from every corner of the earth have asked, "What is this trying to tell me?" That question is the starting point of all symbolic systems.

What's interesting is that these systems often echo each other, even when separated by continents or centuries. A black cat might be a symbol of bad luck in one tradition and spiritual power in another. The moon might represent the feminine, the subconscious, or the cycle of death and rebirth, depending on where you look—but the moon is always meaningful. Patterns like these show us that the language of signs is not fixed, but layered. It has universal elements and local interpretations.

This is why trying to impose one rigid definition on any sign can limit your understanding. A snake might mean danger, healing, temptation, or transformation, depending on the context. In Christianity, it might symbolize evil. In Hinduism, it can represent divine energy. In shamanic cultures, it's a powerful guide of rebirth. None of these meanings are wrong. They reflect different ways of relating to the same symbol.

So when you're trying to interpret signs, it helps to understand the culture or belief system that shaped them. But it's even more important to explore how they resonate with you. Cultural background, religious upbringing, and personal experience all influence what a sign means to you specifically. Meaning is both inherited and personal. And when it comes to decoding signs, both matter.

This is why signs are not just about language or tradition. They are a dialogue between the world and the individual. One person might see a hawk and feel watched over. Another might see the same hawk and feel a warning. The truth is not in the bird. It's in the connection between the moment, the observer, and the emotion it stirs.

To ignore the cultural layers of signs is to miss their richness. But to blindly follow cultural interpretations without checking your own inner response is to give up your authority. The path of discerning signs is about both learning and feeling. It's where the ancestral and the intuitive meet.

This meeting point between collective wisdom and individual insight is where the real power of signs lies. You are not a passive receiver of ancient codes. You are an active interpreter. When a sign appears, it's not only shaped by thousands of years of human meaning-making—it's also filtered through your own story, your own energy, your own present-moment awareness.

The world doesn't whisper in just one language. It speaks in layers. And it's up to you to listen with more than just your intellect. You listen with your whole being. You notice the timing of the event. You check in with your emotions. You ask what else is happening around you. You explore what the sign might mean within the framework of your spiritual or cultural lens, and then you sit quietly with the part that resonates most deeply.

That resonance is the key. You may study the traditional meanings of a symbol, but if it lands flat, it's probably not for you. On the other hand, if something stirs in your chest or brings a deep sense of knowing—even if you can't explain it—that's a signal to pay closer attention. Your intuition is a valid decoder.

Some people feel uncomfortable with this kind of flexibility. They want a fixed dictionary of signs, a list of guaranteed meanings. But signs are alive. They adapt to the moment. They interact with you. They are less like labels and more like mirrors. The same image might reflect different truths at different times, depending on what you need to see.

This is why humility is so important in this work. You are not trying to master some rigid code. You're cultivating sensitivity. You're becoming someone who notices. Someone who reflects. Someone who allows the world to speak in its own language, without rushing to force conclusions. It also means recognizing the role of bias. Just as signs are filtered through your intuition, they can also be distorted by fear, hope, or unresolved emotion. A coincidence might feel like a sign because you desperately want it to be. A warning might be ignored because it's inconvenient. That's why ongoing self-awareness is part of learning this language. The clearer your internal world becomes, the cleaner your perception of external signals.

Cross-cultural understanding can support that clarity. Learning how signs operate in other traditions can expand your symbolic vocabulary and free you from the narrow assumptions of your own upbringing. You may discover, for instance, that what your culture calls bad luck is seen elsewhere as a sign of powerful transformation. You may realize that your recurring dream of a snake has roots in multiple traditions, all of which point toward shedding, healing, and rebirth.

This broader view doesn't dilute meaning. It deepens it. It reminds you that you're part of a much bigger human experience. You're not just interpreting signs for your own benefit. You're stepping into an ancient practice that connects you to others through time and space.

It also gives you the freedom to choose what frameworks empower you. If one system of belief limits your growth or instills fear, you don't have to stay inside it. The wisdom of signs is not about control. It's about awakening. It's about recognizing that the world is alive with meaning, and that you are capable of reading it—not through superstition, but through awareness and alignment.

You are not meant to walk through life blindfolded, hoping for clarity. The signs are there. The systems exist. The question is whether you're willing to trust yourself to see beyond habit, to think beyond dogma, and to let the world show you what it has been trying to say all along.

Let's keep going. You're learning to read the map that was always there—etched in moments, symbols, and synchronicities. You're remembering a language that was never fully lost.

Why the Universe Communicates Through Symbols

If you've ever had a dream you couldn't shake, noticed a number repeating everywhere you looked, or felt an unexplainable pull toward a certain image or phrase, you've brushed up against the symbolic language of the universe. But why does the universe speak this way? Why not send messages in direct, literal words? Why symbols?

The answer lies in the nature of how we perceive reality and how consciousness itself operates. The human mind is not just a rational processor of information. It's also an emotional and intuitive receiver. Symbols bypass the surface layers of logic and reach straight into the unconscious mind—the part of you that processes patterns, feelings, and meaning long before words are formed. This is the language of dreams, myths, and deep insight. It's not about clarity in the way we usually define it. It's about resonance.

Symbols allow communication on multiple levels at once. A word has one definition. A symbol can contain layers. A raven might represent death in one moment, transformation in another, and ancestral presence in yet another—depending on what is needed. This flexibility is part of the design. It meets you where you are, without demanding that the message conform to strict definitions.

This is also why different people can receive different meanings from the same symbol. The universe speaks in symbols because it's not just transmitting information. It's co-creating experience. It's not giving you instructions from the outside. It's inviting you into a dialogue that reflects who you are, what you're becoming, and how open you are to seeing the deeper currents at play in your life.

Think about how we use symbols in daily life. A heart emoji doesn't just mean "heart." It can carry affection, appreciation, comfort, or love. Its meaning depends on context. The same is true for universal signs. A coin on the sidewalk might be a simple object, or it might remind you of abundance, affirmation, or a loved one who used to collect them. The power is not in the object itself. It's in what it activates in you.

That's the secret: symbols open a doorway into meaning that is personal, alive, and often mysterious. They create space for reflection, for intuition, for insight that doesn't have to be explained right away. In a world that's always pushing for fast answers and rigid logic, the symbolic path slows you down. It asks you to feel, to observe, to be curious instead of certain.

The universe communicates this way because it honors your freedom. Literal commands leave no room for interpretation. But symbols offer choice. They nudge rather than push. They suggest rather than demand. You are not forced into belief. You're invited into awareness. You decide what meaning to take, what to investigate further, and what to let go.

This is not some cryptic or inaccessible form of communication reserved for mystics. It's embedded in how we think, how we remember, and how we grow. From childhood stories to sacred rituals, from advertising to personal dreams, we are constantly decoding symbols. The difference is whether we do it with intention—or miss the opportunity entirely.

Symbols also help us bypass the noise. In a world filled with constant notifications, information overload, and mental chatter, symbolic messages have a way of cutting through. A number you keep seeing on license plates. A song that plays the moment you start doubting yourself. A bird landing in front of you just when you're about to make a big decision. These aren't full paragraphs of explanation. They're brief flashes of clarity that slip past mental resistance and land directly where they're needed.

This is part of their intelligence. Symbols don't need to convince you. They don't argue. They show up, subtle and persistent, until you notice. And once you do, your awareness starts to shift. You begin to listen differently. You start asking new questions, ones that go beyond logic and move into meaning. The conversation opens.

Many spiritual traditions have always known this. Indigenous cultures, ancient civilizations, and even modern psychological systems like Jungian analysis all place great importance on the symbolic. Not because it's vague, but because it's precise in a different way. It speaks to the soul, not just the intellect. It doesn't need to be justified. It just needs to be felt.

There's also a practical reason behind this symbolic design: symbols are timeless and culture-spanning. Words can become outdated or mistranslated. A specific phrase might mean one thing in one language and something completely different in another. But a tree, a flame, the moon, a spiral, an eye—these show up across centuries and continents. They carry archetypal weight, meaning that resonates across human experience. The universe uses symbols because they last. They travel. They connect.

At the same time, symbols evolve with you. A symbol you once associated with fear can later become a mark of growth. A color that meant caution in one phase of life might start to mean strength in another. That's the beauty of symbolic language—it's alive. It adapts to who you are now, while still echoing layers of what it meant before. This allows for personal transformation to be mirrored in the signs you receive.

But none of this works without presence. To receive symbols as communication, you have to be attuned. Distracted living makes symbolic language invisible. You can't decode a message you never noticed. That's why the first step in any symbolic dialogue is awareness. Not obsessive searching, but grounded openness. The willingness to pause. To pay attention. To recognize when something moves you or pulls at your attention in a way that doesn't make sense on the surface.

From there, you build fluency. Not through memorizing universal meanings, but through developing your own intuitive language. This is not about looking up every feather or animal in a book. It's about learning how your life speaks to you. What symbols show up in your dreams? What patterns emerge in moments of clarity? What images repeat in your meditations or your journal entries? These are not random. They're threads, waiting to be followed.

Ultimately, symbols help us bridge the seen and unseen. They offer a way to connect the dots between what's happening in our physical world and what's moving beneath the surface. They make the invisible visible, not through explanation, but through experience. And they do it in a way that honors both mystery and meaning. The universe isn't trying to confuse you. It's trying to invite you deeper. Symbols are the doorways. What matters is not that you interpret every symbol "correctly." What matters is that you respond. That you listen. That you allow space for a conversation to unfold—one that can guide you, comfort you, challenge you, and ultimately, align you with something greater than yourself.

Chapter 2: Why You've Been Missing the Signs

The Noise That Drowns Out Spiritual Signals

Before you can truly hear a signal, you have to notice the interference. Modern life is full of it. The hum of constant connectivity. The endless scroll of opinions, updates, and advertising. Notifications pinging your phone before you've even had a chance to finish your thoughts. The pressure to be productive, informed, validated, and entertained—all at once—has created an internal environment where subtlety struggles to survive.

Spiritual signals are not delivered through chaos. They are rarely loud. They don't compete for your attention the way news headlines or social media do. They whisper. They arrive in quiet nudges, soft impressions, gentle repetitions. They move beneath the surface of conscious thought, waiting for a moment of stillness to make themselves known. But in a world trained to reward stimulation and noise, stillness is often drowned out.

It's not just digital noise. There's emotional and psychological clutter too. Worry. Self-doubt. Overthinking. Constant mental rehearsals of worst-case scenarios. The running commentary of comparison, criticism, and internal pressure that loops in the background of your daily life. These aren't just mood states—they act like static, interfering with your ability to tune in. When the mind is loud and reactive, your ability to sense something deeper becomes muted.

Cultural conditioning adds another layer. Many of us were taught that rational thinking is the only valid mode of knowing. That if you can't measure it, explain it, or back it up with data, it doesn't count. This mindset is useful in many areas of life—but it also creates a blind spot. It dismisses intuition as unreliable. It treats gut feelings like distractions. And it subtly trains us to ignore the very signals that could offer clarity, peace, and deeper alignment.

Then there's busyness. Constant motion. Days packed to the edges. When you're rushing from one task to another, your body might be present, but your awareness isn't. It's already on the next thing. You move through life without pausing long enough to register what's trying to reach you. You miss the signs not because they're not there, but because there's no room to notice them.

Even well-meaning habits can contribute to the noise. An over-reliance on external guidance—whether through podcasts, books, or advice from others—can replace your own inner listening. Spiritual signals are not about outsourcing your truth. They're about deepening your relationship with it. But if your attention is always directed outward, you may lose touch with the language your life is trying to speak to you directly.

You can't eliminate all noise. The goal isn't to run away from the world or live in silence. The goal is discernment. It's about creating inner spaciousness—pockets of quiet, moments of reflection, boundaries with distraction—so that the subtle becomes audible again. Signals don't require force to be heard. They require presence.

Creating that space doesn't mean changing everything overnight. It begins with noticing the noise. Not judging it. Not trying to banish it completely. Just becoming aware of what fills your mind and environment, and asking yourself if it's helping you hear, or making it harder. That simple awareness is a turning point. It's the start of a different kind of listening.

This kind of inner awareness doesn't require silence in your environment, only space in your attention. A single moment of full presence—when you're not multi-tasking or mentally rushing—can reveal insights that hours of effort cannot. It might show up while you're walking, washing dishes, or simply staring out a window. The moment you create just a little internal stillness, the signal often emerges from behind the static.

That's why practices like mindfulness, meditation, breathwork, and even conscious pauses throughout the day aren't luxuries. They are recalibration tools. They help retune your inner frequencies so you can differentiate between internal noise and genuine insight. The signal isn't missing. It's waiting for you to clear the bandwidth.

It's also helpful to notice what specifically increases your internal noise. Is it certain conversations? A particular type of media? Rushing your morning routine? Skipping breaks? Everyone has different patterns, but most people aren't aware of them until they stop and pay attention. When you can identify your personal sources of interference, you gain agency. You can start adjusting the volume on your life.

You might find that it's not just external input, but internal resistance that's crowding the space. Many people say they want signs, but deep down they fear what those signs might reveal. If something in you is afraid to see or afraid to act on what you might see, that fear becomes part of the noise. Denial, avoidance, or hesitation creates a kind of emotional interference that filters what you're willing to register. The deeper your honesty, the clearer your reception.

It takes courage to quiet the noise. It's easier to stay distracted than to face what's unresolved. But the clarity you gain is worth more than the comfort of staying unconscious. Once you begin to hear the signal— once you start noticing synchronicities, symbolic patterns, intuitive nudges—you'll wonder how you ever lived in that storm of static without realizing how much you were missing.

This clarity is not just spiritual. It has practical consequences. It sharpens your decision-making. It strengthens your confidence in your own intuition. It helps you recognize when something is in alignment or out of integrity. It allows you to act from a place of centered knowing instead of reactive guessing. That alone changes everything. Relationships, work, purpose, peace—all of it becomes clearer when the noise stops dictating the terms of your awareness.

You don't have to eliminate every distraction, but you do have to take responsibility for how much space you allow them to occupy. You don't have to meditate for hours, but you do need to create small, consistent pauses that allow for stillness. You don't have to chase signs, but you do need to be quiet enough to notice them when they arrive.

The universe doesn't compete for your attention. It waits for your presence. It speaks in a language that favors the attuned. By choosing to step away from noise, even briefly, you're not losing momentum— you're gaining clarity. That clarity is what lets the signal come through. Not louder, but clearer. Not more frequent, but more recognizable.

And once you start hearing it, you begin to trust it. Not because it always gives you easy answers, but because it reconnects you to something deeper than the noise: the part of you that remembers how to listen.

Modern Conditioning and the Loss of Inner Awareness

Most people today are walking around with a muted sense of inner awareness, not because they lack intuition, but because they've been conditioned out of it. From an early age, we are trained to prioritize logic over instinct, external validation over internal truth, and speed over reflection. This training is so widespread and normalized that many don't even realize it happened. They assume their disconnection is personal when in fact it's cultural.

Consider the structure of modern life. From school to work, almost everything is measured by output, performance, and quantifiable success. There's little room for silence, stillness, or intuitive processing. Even rest has become something to optimize, tracked by apps and tied to productivity. In such a system, inner awareness isn't just neglected— it's actively suppressed.

Children often display a natural sensitivity to subtle cues, both emotional and energetic. They notice when something feels off, even if they can't articulate it. They follow curiosity instinctively. But over time, they're taught to override those signals. "Don't be silly." "That's just your imagination." "There's no reason to feel that way." These kinds of comments, though often well-meaning, teach them to mistrust their inner guidance. The result? Adults who no longer recognize the language of their own soul.

Technology amplifies the problem. We live in a world where constant connectivity is celebrated, where moments of boredom are filled with scrolling, and where attention is divided into fragments. This hyper-stimulation creates a fragmented mind, one that struggles to stay anchored in the present moment. Inner awareness can't compete with a stream of digital noise unless we deliberately create space for it.

Our cultural bias toward rationality also plays a role. We've been conditioned to believe that only what can be measured, tested, or proven holds value. But inner awareness doesn't fit neatly into scientific frameworks. It's subtle. It's experiential. It often defies logic, appearing in the form of feelings, symbols, dreams, or sudden knowing. When this kind of perception arises, it's often dismissed as irrational, even by the people experiencing it. They second-guess themselves, not because they're wrong, but because they've been trained to doubt what can't be explained.

There's also a societal fear of vulnerability. Inner awareness often brings us into contact with feelings that aren't convenient—grief, confusion, longing, or unresolved wounds. Tuning in might mean facing something uncomfortable. And in a culture that promotes numbing over processing, distraction over confrontation, it's easier to stay outwardly busy than to risk opening the door to those deeper layers.

What we lose in this process is more than intuition. We lose the thread of connection between ourselves and the larger intelligence that speaks through signs, synchronicities, and the language of energy. We stop noticing the symbolic patterns that once guided us. We ignore our body's signals. We override gut feelings. We accept a narrowed version of reality that excludes the unseen.

But the ability to tune back in is not gone. It's just buried. Like a radio station playing beneath static, your inner awareness is still transmitting. Reclaiming it doesn't require becoming someone new—it requires unlearning the noise. This means examining the assumptions you've absorbed about what counts as "real" or "useful." It means giving yourself permission to value the invisible. It means creating pauses in your day, even just a few breaths, where you stop performing and simply listen.

The rebuilding process starts with attention. Not forced focus, but soft awareness. Most people expect intuition to shout over the noise of their day, but it doesn't. It waits. It whispers. And the more you practice tuning in, the clearer it becomes. This doesn't require a complete life overhaul. It starts with noticing. Noticing how you feel when you walk into a room. Noticing when something feels slightly off or strangely aligned. Noticing when your body tightens in response to a choice or relaxes in relief. These are the breadcrumbs back to inner awareness.

Yet noticing alone isn't enough. You also need to believe what you notice. The mind, conditioned by years of skepticism and social reinforcement, will often dismiss your internal impressions. You'll second-guess yourself. You'll tell yourself you're imagining things. But each time you pause and choose to trust your internal signal, you loosen the grip of conditioning. You prove to yourself that your inner voice still works.

Another layer of conditioning that must be dismantled is the addiction to certainty. Modern culture often rewards black-and-white thinking. We're taught to choose sides, have clear answers, and dismiss ambiguity. But inner awareness thrives in the in-between. It's not always immediate. It doesn't always come with explanations. You may get a nudge without a reason. A sense of timing without a clock. This ambiguity can feel uncomfortable until you learn to see it as part of the process. The goal is not always clarity, but attunement.

Cultural conditioning also teaches people to externalize authority. They look to experts, systems, or influencers to tell them what to do, how to feel, and what to believe. And while there's value in external learning, it's dangerous when it replaces internal knowing. No one else lives inside your body. No one else carries your exact blueprint. What feels right to you, even if no one else understands it, matters. Rebuilding inner awareness means reclaiming your place as your own authority—not from arrogance, but from trust.

One of the most powerful tools for reawakening this trust is stillness. In stillness, distractions fade and deeper layers surface. But stillness is not just about meditation. It can be a walk without your phone, a moment of silence before you speak, or the decision to listen instead of fill space. These are small acts, but they create cracks in the armor of conditioning. They let truth seep in.

Emotionally, many people have been taught to override their feelings. If you're sensitive, you were likely told to toughen up. If you're emotional, you might have been labeled dramatic. But sensitivity is not weakness. It's perception. It means you're attuned to shifts others may miss. Reconnecting with your feelings is part of reclaiming your inner map. Emotions are messengers, not obstacles. When allowed to move through you, they often carry intuitive insight that can't be accessed through thought alone.

This reconditioning takes time, not because the process is slow, but because unlearning happens in layers. It's not a single realization, but a series of subtle recognitions that accumulate into transformation. You'll start to notice what you used to ignore. You'll start to pause before reacting. You'll sense things before they happen. And in those moments, you'll realize you never really lost your awareness—it was just buried beneath layers you didn't know were there.

This is not about returning to some idealized past. It's about choosing to live from the inside out. When you restore your connection to your inner signals, you begin to live with a different kind of intelligence. One that is not loud, but wise. Not analytical, but clear. And it is in that clarity that the language of the universe begins to come alive again.

How to Start Tuning In Again

Tuning back in to the subtle language of the universe is not about adopting complex rituals or following rigid spiritual routines. It's about returning to something natural—something that was always there, just quieted by distraction, pressure, and noise. You already have the capacity to notice signs and feel intuitive nudges. The work lies in creating the internal and external space where those signals can come through again. The first step is learning to recognize the difference between inner stillness and mental emptiness. Many people try to "quiet their minds" only to find themselves frustrated by constant thought loops. But tuning in doesn't require a blank mind. It requires presence. You can have thoughts and still be present. You can sit in silence without forcing yourself to stop thinking. The key is to observe without attachment. When you allow thoughts to pass like clouds rather than clinging to each one, you begin to drop below the surface level of mental chatter.

This state of relaxed presence is the fertile ground where signs begin to appear more clearly. It's not something that needs to be forced or dramatized. You simply become a little more available to what's already there. A flicker of emotion. A strange coincidence. A physical sensation you would normally ignore. These moments begin to stand out when your nervous system is not in constant overdrive.

To reach this state more consistently, your nervous system must feel safe. That's something most people don't associate with spiritual sensitivity, but it's essential. If your body is in survival mode—whether from stress, trauma, or overstimulation—it's much harder to notice subtle messages. Your energy is focused on coping, not connecting. So the practical foundation of tuning in is creating an environment, both inside and outside yourself, where you don't feel the need to be on alert all the time.

This might mean reducing digital noise. It might mean stepping away from people or environments that constantly trigger anxiety or urgency. It might mean building small, nourishing rituals that signal to your body that you are safe, grounded, and open. These are not indulgences. They are necessary conditions for reconnection.

Next comes awareness of rhythm. Your life already has a rhythm, even if it feels chaotic. There are times you feel more open and others when you feel shut down. There are hours when your mind is clear and others when you're foggy. Start to observe when you naturally feel more in tune with yourself. Is it early in the morning, before the world wakes up? Is it late at night, when the day's demands have fallen away? Finding and honoring your personal rhythm is a gentle but powerful way to rebuild intuitive access.

At this stage, it's also helpful to reengage with your body as a tool for perception, not just function. You've likely been trained to see your body as something to manage—through fitness, appearance, performance. But the body is also a sensing system. It reacts to energy long before the conscious mind processes it. You might feel a tightening in your stomach, a pull in your chest, or a tingling on your skin in response to someone or something. These are not random. They are signals.

Many people override these sensations because they don't fit into rational explanation. But part of tuning in again is learning to trust those first impressions. The body often speaks before words arrive. To access that language, slow down enough to listen.

When you give yourself that space to listen, subtle messages start to surface more frequently. Patterns you used to brush off suddenly stand out. You begin to notice that every time you ignore a gut feeling, something goes off track. Or that when you follow an instinct without overthinking, things unfold more smoothly. These are not coincidences. They are proof that your inner guidance system is active and waiting to be used.

One of the most effective ways to sharpen this system is through reflective attention. This doesn't mean overanalyzing everything you experience, but it does mean setting aside a few minutes each day to check in. Ask yourself: What stood out to me today? Was there a strange moment, a repeated phrase, a number I kept seeing, or a feeling I couldn't shake? Write it down without trying to make sense of it immediately. The point isn't to decode everything right away. The point is to show your mind that you're paying attention.

Over time, this habit builds an internal feedback loop. When your mind knows that you will pause and reflect, it begins to highlight what matters. Your awareness sharpens, not by force, but by attention. You start to notice not just what's loud and obvious, but what's quiet and persistent. These are often the most meaningful signs—the ones that don't demand your attention but wait patiently for you to notice.

Another layer of reconnection involves the environment around you. Nature has always been a medium through which spiritual signs are communicated. Not because trees and birds are magical in themselves, but because nature operates on a rhythm that is ancient and uninterrupted. Spending even a few minutes a day outside, watching how light moves through leaves or how the wind shifts the space around you, begins to recalibrate your internal rhythm. You remember how to listen without an agenda.

As this practice deepens, you'll likely notice an emotional shift. Instead of looking for signs as validation or answers, you begin to recognize them as part of an ongoing dialogue. You stop trying to control the outcome and become more interested in what is being revealed to you, piece by piece. This shift from control to curiosity is essential. It moves you from a transactional mindset to a relational one, where you're not trying to make the universe prove something to you. You're learning how to stay in conversation with it.

That conversation is not always logical or linear. It often unfolds through layers—one dream, one encounter, one sensation at a time. It requires trust. Not blind faith, but grounded trust in your own experience. If something feels significant, honor that feeling. If something keeps recurring, don't dismiss it. You're not being superstitious. You're building fluency in a symbolic language that doesn't always speak in complete sentences.

To support this process, simplicity matters. You don't need elaborate rituals, expensive tools, or perfect conditions. What you need is consistency, presence, and a willingness to slow down. Five minutes of true attention are more powerful than an hour of distracted searching. One genuine moment of inner stillness can reset your connection more deeply than any technique.

In the end, tuning in is not about becoming someone else. It's about remembering who you were before the noise took over. Before you were taught to dismiss your instincts or to mistrust the unknown. The universe has always been speaking to you. Your job now is to meet it halfway—not with desperation, but with quiet readiness. That's how the dialogue begins again.

Chapter 3: The Three Sources of Spiritual Signs

External Signs: Nature, Numbers, Events

Some of the most powerful messages from the universe do not arrive as words or visions. They come from the outside world, disguised as ordinary moments. A sudden shift in weather, a bird landing near you and staring longer than usual, a strange series of numbers that repeat across clocks, license plates, receipts. These are not always random. When viewed with attention, they can reveal patterns that speak directly to your life.

Nature is one of the most ancient channels of spiritual communication. Long before organized religion, our ancestors read the skies, watched the movements of animals, and felt the rhythms of the earth. These were not just primitive survival tools. They were a living dialogue with the environment. Even now, despite our technology and fast-paced routines, nature hasn't stopped speaking. We've just stopped listening.

When something in nature catches your attention without you seeking it, take note. Maybe a certain animal keeps crossing your path, or a particular flower blooms earlier than expected. Perhaps a tree you walk by every day suddenly seems to "stand out" in an unexplainable way. The significance often lies not in the object itself, but in the context of your own life. What were you thinking about at the moment? What question has been on your heart lately? The natural world often responds to the energy you emit, reflecting back images or patterns that align with your inner state.

Weather is another form of external signaling. It's not just about whether it's sunny or raining. It's about noticing when a sudden shift in atmosphere mirrors a change inside of you. Maybe you're feeling overwhelmed, and a dense fog settles over your town. Maybe you've made a major decision, and the sky opens in a burst of light just as you step outside. While some may see these as coincidences, others understand them as synchronistic reflections of the invisible threads connecting our inner and outer worlds.

Then there are numbers. Repeating sequences like 111, 222, 444, and 11:11 are often called "angel numbers," but labels aside, the key is that they seem to show up precisely when something is stirring inside you. It's not about superstition. It's about noticing when the fabric of reality briefly reveals a pattern, as if nudging you to pay attention. These numbers don't always have universal meanings. What matters most is what they mean to you in the moment they appear.

For example, maybe you're doubting a new direction, and you glance at the clock at 5:55. That repetition becomes a pause. It interrupts your mental spiral and invites reflection. Numbers that repeat can act like punctuation marks in your day. They don't speak in full sentences, but they signal emphasis. They can mark turning points, affirm decisions, or call for reassessment.

Beyond nature and numbers, life events themselves can function as signs. Unexpected delays, accidents, or perfect timing are not always just luck or misfortune. Sometimes, a closed door is a message. Sometimes, a person missing the bus changes the entire outcome of their day. The more conscious you become, the more you start to see how the timing of events feels orchestrated rather than random.

What matters is the resonance. When something external feels charged with meaning, it is. That doesn't mean every event is preordained, or that we must live in a constant state of decoding. It means staying open, aware, and willing to see patterns when they emerge, rather than dismissing them out of habit.

A helpful shift happens when you begin to see life less as a sequence of unrelated moments and more as a dialogue. You do not need to strain or force interpretation. The clearest signs often feel simple, obvious, even slightly surreal. You feel it in your body before your mind catches up. A chill up your spine. A pause in your breath. A sense that something just aligned in a way that words can't explain.

This is especially true with repeated occurrences. Seeing the same symbol three times in a day, hearing the same phrase from unrelated people, running into a stranger who reminds you of a forgotten goal. These are all examples of layered messages. They are not isolated signs, but echoing signals that invite you to look beneath the surface. The more frequent the repetition, the more likely there is something there for you to notice. The challenge is not in seeing these patterns, but in trusting them. We are taught to value logic over intuition, data over feeling. So when something meaningful shows up in a non-linear way, we second-guess it. We assume it must be a coincidence, or that we're just reading too much into it. But that very doubt is part of the conditioning that dulls our inner perception.

It's important to stay grounded while also remaining receptive. Not every delay is a cosmic message. Not every number is a prophecy. But when something pierces through your normal awareness, when it disrupts your routine in a way that feels oddly personal, take note. Even if the meaning isn't immediately clear, your attention itself creates space for clarity to emerge.

In this process, timing plays a crucial role. A sign that would seem meaningless on one day can feel deeply significant on another, simply because of what you're carrying internally. That's why signs are not objective truths, but relational messages. They meet you where you are. The same number or image might mean something entirely different to someone else. What matters is your own energetic state, your questions, your intentions.

One way to strengthen your ability to perceive these external signs is to cultivate stillness. The quieter your internal world becomes, the more you notice the subtle movements around you. You become less reactive and more observant. Your environment begins to mirror your thoughts in ways that feel unmistakable. Not because reality is suddenly different, but because your perception has shifted.

Eventually, this heightened awareness becomes a way of life. You stop needing dramatic signs because you've learned to read the small ones. A breeze at the right moment. A sentence overheard that answers your private question. A license plate that reminds you of someone you miss. These are not distractions. They are alignments. Nudges. Clues that you are not as alone or directionless as you sometimes fear.

The more you honor these moments, the more they show up. Not because the universe is testing you, but because you are finally listening. Your attention is the invitation. Your presence is the key that unlocks the pattern. The signals are already there. You are the one learning to see.

Internal Signs: Emotion, Intuition, and Dreams

Not all signs are external. Some of the clearest signals come from within, quietly whispering beneath the noise of daily life. These internal signs are often dismissed, yet they carry the most personalized form of guidance. Emotions, gut instincts, and dreams are not random byproducts of the mind. They are intelligent responses that emerge from deep layers of your inner world. Learning to listen to them with curiosity and trust can shift your relationship with life itself.

Start with emotion. We're taught to see emotions as reactions to circumstances, but they're also indicators of deeper alignment or misalignment. A sudden sense of unease, even in a seemingly safe situation, may be pointing you toward something important. A wave of peace while thinking about a specific decision may not be just relief, but a deeper confirmation. Emotions often know what the conscious mind has not yet understood. They carry the resonance of truth long before facts line up.

Most people are trained to suppress or rationalize emotions. They explain them away or try to "get over them" instead of sitting with them. But emotional signals are less about right and wrong, and more about congruence. When something feels off, even slightly, that's worth listening to. You don't need immediate answers. You just need awareness. Emotional patterns that arise repeatedly around certain people, places, or choices are especially worth tracking. The consistency of those feelings is a signal in itself.

Then there's intuition. Unlike emotion, intuition is quieter, less charged. It doesn't shout. It nudges. You might feel it as a subtle pull in a certain direction, or a clear knowing that bypasses logic. It often arrives without explanation, but with a strong sense of accuracy. When you've ignored your intuition in the past, you've likely noticed that events confirmed it later. This pattern teaches that intuition is not random or whimsical. It's a refined sensory system, one that functions best when not drowned out by doubt or overthinking.

Many intuitive impressions come as physical sensations. A tightness in the chest. A clenching in the stomach. A sudden energy shift. These are not just stress responses. They're often your body's way of saying, "Something here matters." Over time, you can begin to decode the language of these sensations. What does a light, expansive feeling signal for you? What does a sharp drop in energy mean in certain contexts? These patterns are as real and reliable as any external cue, once you learn their meanings.

Dreams, meanwhile, open an entirely different realm of internal signaling. The dream state bypasses the filters of the waking mind. It gives direct access to the subconscious, where messages are delivered in images, metaphors, and symbolic sequences. While not every dream is profound, some carry unmistakable emotional weight or strange clarity. These are the ones to pay attention to.

Sometimes a dream offers a solution to a waking problem. Other times, it brings back emotions or memories you've buried. And occasionally, a dream shows you something that hasn't happened yet, but feels charged with truth. This doesn't mean you need to interpret every detail. Instead, notice what stands out. The feeling tone. The central symbol. The unresolved action. Often, these elements mirror something in your waking life that's trying to surface.

Many people dismiss dreams as meaningless because they don't understand them. But meaning doesn't need to be fully understood to be valuable. A dream that leaves you feeling awakened, disturbed, or inspired is already doing its job. It's inviting you into a deeper conversation with yourself.

The key is not to analyze dreams like puzzles, but to relate to them as messages in a different language. Keep a record, even of fragments. Patterns often appear over time, and symbols that seem strange at first can begin to carry personal meaning. A recurring staircase might represent progress. A certain person might reflect an inner trait you're avoiding or awakening. These are not fixed interpretations. They are mirrors that help you notice where your energy is trying to go.

Internal signs often arise during stillness, when the outside world quiets enough for the inner world to speak. But in modern life, that stillness is rare. Screens, schedules, and constant stimulation crowd the space where intuitive and emotional awareness would naturally surface. This is why practices like journaling, meditative walking, or simply spending time alone in nature are not luxuries. They are access points. Without them, the signal is still there, but buried under too much noise.

Sometimes internal signs show up not through new insights, but through discomfort. Resistance, anxiety, or fatigue can all carry messages. Not every signal feels good. But a sense of friction in your inner world often means something is misaligned. Perhaps you've said yes when your body said no. Or ignored a subtle knowing that was trying to get your attention. That inner tension is guidance in disguise. Rather than pushing through it, try becoming curious. What is this feeling trying to redirect?

It's also important to trust that your internal compass doesn't need to match anyone else's. One person might receive intuitive signals through emotion, another through sensation, another through thought. Some people feel a shift in body temperature when something is meaningful. Others experience flashes of insight that feel like they came from nowhere. What matters most is learning your own system. Becoming fluent in the way your own body and mind communicate truth to you.

This process takes patience and presence. There is no instant formula. But every time you choose to notice, to pause instead of override, you're strengthening that connection. You're saying to your deeper self: I'm listening now. And that opens the door for more clarity, more consistency, and more trust in what you receive.

You'll likely notice that as your sensitivity increases, these internal signs begin to synchronize with external ones. You feel a pull toward something, and then a confirmation arrives in the form of a meaningful coincidence. You dream of someone you haven't seen in years, and they suddenly reach out. These are not just curious events. They are reflections of your alignment. When inner and outer signals begin to echo each other, you know you're tuned in.

But even when there is no external match, internal signs are enough. Your intuition is not less valid just because it can't be explained. Your emotions are not irrational just because others don't feel them. Your dreams are not insignificant just because they don't make perfect sense. These are deep, personal forms of communication. They require trust more than proof.

Ultimately, learning to receive and respect internal signs is about reclaiming authority over your own experience. It means no longer outsourcing your clarity to external sources, but remembering that the deepest wisdom often comes from within. You already carry the compass. You already have access to insight, even before the world reflects it back. When you build that inner relationship with care, you start moving through life with a different kind of confidence. Not the kind that knows every answer, but the kind that knows where to listen.

This is not just about tuning in. It's about remembering that you were never disconnected. Only distracted. The signals have always been there, waiting for your attention.

Higher Guidance: Divine, Ancestral, and Collective

There are moments in life when guidance arrives in a form that feels larger than us. A sudden clarity in the middle of confusion. A deep knowing that cuts through fear. A message from a dream that seems to come from someone who is no longer alive. These experiences point to a deeper network of intelligence that transcends the individual mind. They reflect what many spiritual traditions have called higher guidance.

Higher guidance can appear in many forms. Sometimes it feels like divine intervention, other times like a whisper from an ancestor, or even a wave of collective emotion that seems to pass through the entire atmosphere. It is not limited to a single belief system. People from vastly different cultures and backgrounds describe moments of connection with something beyond themselves that brings insight, comfort, or direction. While the language we use to describe it may differ, the core experience is shared.

The idea of divine guidance refers to communication from a higher spiritual intelligence, often personalized and protective in nature. Whether one calls it God, Source, Spirit, or simply the universe, this form of guidance is often experienced as sacred. It's the quiet voice that urges you to take a different path at the last moment. The overwhelming sense of peace during crisis. The prayer answered not in the form you expected, but in the form you needed. This is not about superstition. It's about recognizing patterns of benevolent intervention that invite us to trust a deeper unfolding.

Some people encounter this through prayer or meditation. Others sense it while being still in nature or during moments of creative flow. The experience itself is hard to describe, but it's almost always marked by a sense of presence. You feel accompanied. You feel seen. You feel that you are not alone in your questions or choices.

Ancestral guidance, by contrast, carries a different flavor. It often comes with a feeling of warmth, protection, or remembrance. This form of insight may emerge through dreams, symbols, or synchronicities that seem to echo your lineage. It might be a sudden sense that a grandparent is near, even if you never met them. Or a repeated sign connected to your cultural roots, surfacing just when you need it most.

This type of guidance reminds us that time is not linear in the way we usually perceive it. Those who came before us may still have influence, not through logic or material interaction, but through energetic presence. Many indigenous and traditional cultures hold a deep reverence for ancestors, not as memories, but as active participants in daily life. They are considered part of the living fabric of support, and their wisdom continues to move through generations.

Tuning in to ancestral guidance does not require knowledge of every detail of your family tree. What matters is the openness to receive. If you have a sense of unfinished family stories, unresolved grief, or forgotten strengths, these may surface not just as psychological themes but as invitations to reconnect with the wisdom that lives in your bloodline.

Collective guidance, on the other hand, operates on a larger scale. It is the sense that something is moving through a community, a generation, or even the planet as a whole. It can be felt during times of crisis, transformation, or awakening. There may be a shared mood that everyone seems to pick up on, without speaking it aloud. Or a surge of creativity that sweeps across people in different places at the same time. This form of guidance is less personal, but not less powerful. It often speaks through trends, shared dreams, sudden cultural shifts, or the rise of certain themes in conversation and media. When we tune in to this layer, we start to recognize that we are not thinking in isolation. Our ideas, emotions, and even spiritual questions are connected to a much broader web.

When you begin to recognize collective guidance, it changes how you interpret your own experiences. You start to notice that your thoughts and feelings are not always entirely personal. They are part of a larger energetic current that moves through the world. This is especially true during periods of intense societal change, when emotions like fear, hope, or confusion seem amplified across many people at once. In these moments, your own internal state might be reflecting something much broader, and becoming aware of that distinction can help you stay grounded while staying open.

One way collective guidance reveals itself is through the emergence of symbols or stories that appear across different cultures and contexts, often simultaneously. A specific archetype, number, animal, or theme may show up repeatedly in conversation, media, and art. These are not coincidences to dismiss. They are signals of something that is asking to be seen, felt, and worked through at a global level. Sometimes these patterns arise in response to collective wounds that are ready to be acknowledged. Other times, they point toward shared desires for healing, truth, or evolution.

This interconnected layer of experience can be empowering, especially for those who have felt isolated in their spiritual path. It serves as a reminder that your inner work is not separate from the world around you. When you listen, heal, and grow, you contribute to the larger field of awareness. Your insights ripple outward, just as you are influenced by the quiet ripples of others.

Navigating higher guidance requires discernment. It asks that you listen with more than your ears. It asks that you feel beyond your preferences. Not every strong emotion or intuition is a message from beyond. Not every coincidence holds meaning. Developing discernment means learning to differentiate between your own projections and the presence of real guidance. This requires stillness, honesty, and a willingness to question your assumptions.

Some questions to help with discernment include: Does this guidance feel loving, even if it challenges me? Does it bring a sense of clarity rather than confusion? Is it consistent with the deeper truths I know within myself? Does it encourage growth, responsibility, or connection rather than fear or ego inflation? These are subtle markers that can help you stay aligned with true guidance and avoid being misled by fantasy or anxiety.

Trusting higher guidance also involves surrender. Often, the signs or messages you receive won't come with clear explanations. They may arrive as feelings, images, or synchronicities that only make sense with time. The rational mind might resist this ambiguity, but the heart often understands what the words cannot explain. The more you learn to stay present with the not-knowing, the more you develop the capacity to receive deeper levels of support.

As you build a relationship with divine, ancestral, and collective guidance, you begin to move through the world differently. You pause more often. You pay attention to the moment before you act. You notice how a phrase lands in your body, how a dream leaves an echo in your day, how a stranger's words match something you've been quietly praying about. Life becomes less random and more responsive. Not because every moment is orchestrated, but because you are more attuned to what is speaking through it.

This way of living is not about chasing signs or waiting for permission from beyond. It's about cultivating an inner receptivity that honors the intelligence woven into life itself. The more you respect that intelligence, the more it seems to meet you halfway. And what unfolds is not only guidance, but a deepening intimacy with existence. You begin to feel that life is not only happening around you but also through you, with you, and for you.

This is the silent language of higher guidance. It is not loud or forceful. It arrives with presence. It requires listening. And it is always available when you are ready to receive.

Part II — Decoding the Signs in Real Life

Recognizing that signs exist is only the first step. The real challenge, and the deeper gift, lies in learning how to interpret them. This part of the journey shifts the focus from awareness to understanding. It's where spiritual curiosity meets grounded discernment, and where vague wonder transforms into meaningful clarity. Because signs are not valuable in themselves—they are valuable when they lead us somewhere real.

In everyday life, signs rarely come with clear explanations. They arrive without a manual, coded in symbolism and emotion, filtered through the lens of your personal beliefs and current state of mind. One person might see a repeated number and feel reassurance, while another sees the same pattern and feels anxiety. The difference lies in interpretation. And interpretation is never just about the sign itself—it's also about who you are when you receive it.

This is why decoding signs is not about memorizing meanings from books or looking up fixed definitions online. It is about learning a new way of thinking. It is about becoming someone who can listen inward and observe outward at the same time. Someone who can sit with uncertainty and extract insight without forcing conclusions. Someone who can sense the subtle alignment between inner intuition and outer events, even when logic falls short.

Part II explores the practical art of spiritual interpretation. How do you know if something is meant for you or just noise? How do you differentiate between personal projections and real messages? How do you stay open to signs without becoming superstitious or obsessive? These are not abstract questions. They show up in the decisions you make, the relationships you navigate, and the everyday moments when you feel stuck, unsure, or in need of direction.

This section does not offer formulas. It offers frameworks. Tools to help you reflect, analyze, and trust. It invites you to look at the whole picture instead of grabbing onto isolated pieces. Because real guidance rarely speaks in isolated moments. It speaks through rhythm, through patterns, through echoes that build over time. And when you learn to trace those patterns back to their source, you uncover a dialogue that has been unfolding all along.

Here, decoding is not only about understanding signs—it's about understanding yourself. Your triggers, your filters, your emotional responses, your desires. Every sign you receive passes through the lens of your own psyche. Knowing that lens is essential. Otherwise, it's too easy to misread a message, chase an illusion, or project meaning onto things that were never meant to carry it.

At the same time, decoding does not mean stripping signs of their mystery. You are not trying to solve life like a puzzle. You are learning to live inside the symbols with humility. Sometimes the answer will be clear. Other times, it will unfold over weeks, months, or even years. The more you grow in patience and presence, the more the meanings reveal themselves—not always in words, but often in the shifts they create within you.

Decoding is a practice. A way of relating to life that asks for your full attention. It is about refining your awareness until your inner sense begins to match the outer cues. Not with fear, and not with control, but with trust. This part of the book is your guide to that practice. Not to make you dependent on signs, but to help you build confidence in your ability to read them when they come. Because when you can decode the signs in real life, you stop feeling like the universe is speaking a language you don't understand. You realize it has always been speaking your language. You just needed to remember how to listen.

Chapter 4: The Seven Most Common Types of Signs

Patterns and Repetition

Our minds are designed to find patterns. It's part of our survival instinct. We notice when things repeat because it helps us make sense of the world and predict what might happen next. But not all patterns are created equal. Some are random and meaningless. Others feel charged with significance. The difference lies in how they resonate with us—how they pull at something deeper, triggering a sense that there is a message hidden in the repetition.

Patterns and repetition often act as the universe's highlighters. When something shows up more than once, especially in a short span of time, it draws your attention. A certain word. A phrase. A song. A symbol. A number. A name. A concept. On the surface, it might seem like coincidence. But if you pause and notice what was happening in your life at the exact moment those repetitions occurred, a thread may begin to reveal itself.

The key is not to force meaning, but to become more aware of your emotional state and surroundings when the repetition occurs. Often, a pattern becomes a sign not because of the thing itself, but because of when and how it arrives. Imagine you're questioning a major decision and you keep hearing the word "trust" in different contexts—on a billboard, in a podcast, in a conversation with a stranger. The word may not be remarkable on its own, but its recurrence in moments of uncertainty gives it weight. It's not just the repetition that matters, it's the timing and emotional charge behind it.

Another form of repetition that frequently shows up in spiritual guidance is the recurrence of situations or experiences. Maybe you keep attracting the same type of relationship dynamic, facing the same challenge at work, or having similar emotional reactions to seemingly different events. These are not signs in the traditional sense, but they are patterns that carry a message. They are trying to show you something unresolved or unacknowledged. Until the lesson is learned or the belief behind the pattern is shifted, the repetition will often continue.

These internal and external loops serve as invitations to look deeper. What are you being asked to see? What behavior are you unconsciously repeating? What belief is shaping your choices and experiences? Repetition holds a mirror to your internal landscape. It asks you to slow down, to examine your role in the patterns you encounter, and to consider whether the message is one of healing, change, or confirmation. Not all patterns are obstacles. Some are affirmations. They show up to remind you that you're on the right track, that you're aligned with a higher flow. You might notice the same animals appearing during important transitions, or keep seeing a meaningful number when you're following your intuition. These signs are often subtle, but they bring a sense of peace and quiet certainty. They are less about warning and more about encouragement. You don't need to change direction—you just need to keep going.

There's also something to be said for rhythm. The universe doesn't always speak in isolated events. It speaks in currents. In waves. Repetition can reveal those larger movements. When you begin to track patterns over time, you see more than isolated synchronicities. You start to perceive cycles. Certain themes emerge, dissolve, and return. These rhythms can align with your personal growth, with seasons in your life, or with collective events that affect more than just you. And once you learn to recognize them, you no longer feel like life is random. You begin to trust the tempo of your unfolding.

Recognizing a pattern is only the beginning. The real work is learning how to interpret it without projecting your fears or desires onto it. This requires a grounded inner awareness. You have to be able to ask yourself, "What am I being shown?" rather than "What do I want this to mean?" That shift in perspective can uncover insights you might otherwise miss. Start by asking how the pattern makes you feel. Is there a sense of unease? Comfort? Urgency? Often, the emotional tone of a repeating experience will reveal whether it's calling your attention to a blind spot or offering reassurance. If the pattern feels disruptive or frustrating, it might be challenging you to grow out of an outdated identity or belief. If it feels uplifting or mysteriously reassuring, it might be confirming a step you're afraid to take. The emotional tone is not an answer in itself, but it's a compass.

Pay attention to where the pattern shows up. Is it always tied to a certain person, place, or moment? Does it arise when you are tired, open, vulnerable, or inspired? Patterns often carry context clues, and those clues can help you trace them back to their origin. What belief do they echo? What theme do they reinforce? Sometimes, the same experience repeats in different disguises, but the lesson behind them is identical.

For example, someone might repeatedly find themselves in work environments where their efforts go unrecognized. On the surface, it may seem like a string of bad luck or poor choices. But if you step back and examine the emotional pattern, you might discover a deeper belief: that your value is tied to output, or that you must prove your worth to be seen. Recognizing that belief is the first step to shifting the pattern. Once you acknowledge the inner cause, the outer repetition often begins to dissolve.

There is also a deeper layer to patterns that operate across time. You may notice certain themes revisiting you during specific seasons of the year or even in cycles of several years. This isn't coincidence. Many people experience life as a spiral rather than a straight line. Lessons return in new forms to be understood more fully, not because you've failed, but because you're ready for a deeper layer of awareness. Repetition is not punishment. It's a refinement tool. Each time the pattern returns, you're given a new opportunity to respond differently.

Sometimes, the most profound repetitions are incredibly simple. A friend uses the same phrase you just read in a book. A stranger hums a song you've been dreaming about. You overhear the exact guidance you needed in a place you didn't expect. These are the whispers. They don't demand attention, but they reward it. The more you honor them, the more they seem to increase. And the more they increase, the more your reality begins to feel connected, intentional, alive.

Patterns ask you to be curious. They invite reflection, not obsession. The point is not to become hypervigilant, constantly scanning for meaning in everything, but to adopt a quiet attentiveness. A way of moving through the world that honors your intuition and welcomes symbolic language without becoming consumed by it.

Repetition is one of the most powerful forms of spiritual communication because it teaches through experience. It moves past the rational mind and taps into your inner knowing. When you let go of needing everything to be logical, patterns become doorways. They are not the full message, but they lead you toward it. And over time, with practice and patience, you begin to see not just what is repeating, but why. That is when life begins to shift in subtle, lasting ways. Not because the signs changed, but because you finally learned to read them.

Dreams, Symbols, and Visual Cues

We all dream. Some nights we forget, some nights we remember only fragments, and other nights we wake up as if we've traveled somewhere profound, touched something meaningful, and returned with a whisper we don't quite know how to translate. Dreams have long been regarded as messengers, stretching across every culture, spiritual tradition, and time period. They offer symbols, images, and metaphors that speak not in the language of logic but of inner truth.

What makes dreams particularly powerful is that they bypass the conscious mind. They are not shaped by your ego or your to-do list. They emerge from a deeper place within you, a place more aligned with the intuitive and energetic layers of your being. In this sense, dreams can act like inner signs. They reflect your inner state with incredible honesty. Sometimes they surface unresolved emotions. Other times they offer symbolic previews of what's to come. And occasionally, they deliver precise guidance you didn't even know you needed.

Not every dream carries meaning. Some are simply mental housekeeping. But the ones that linger—the ones that feel vivid, charged, strange, or unusually resonant—those are worth paying attention to. These dreams tend to carry symbolic language. You may not immediately understand why you're walking through a dark hallway or why a certain animal keeps appearing, but something in you knows it matters. These recurring symbols are often more truthful than words. They bypass intellect and speak directly to the subconscious.

Symbols in dreams function similarly to signs in waking life. Their power lies in how they make you feel and in what they trigger in your memory or emotion. For instance, water might appear in a dream when you're facing deep emotional change. It might be a calm lake or a violent ocean, and each version tells a different story. A locked door might represent a part of yourself you haven't accessed. A bird might symbolize perspective or freedom, depending on how it behaves in the dream.

You don't need a dictionary of dream symbols to start interpreting these cues. In fact, relying too much on external definitions can block your own intuitive understanding. The best way to work with symbols is to notice how they resonate with your personal experience. What does that object or setting mean to you, based on your past, your beliefs, your emotions? This is a much more accurate path than assigning a one-size-fits-all meaning to each dream.

Outside of sleep, symbols appear all the time in waking life. The world is full of visual cues that often go unnoticed because we've stopped seeing them. The human mind is trained to filter out what it deems unimportant. It sorts, categorizes, and simplifies reality to reduce overwhelm. But in doing so, it also filters out many signs. A sudden image that draws your attention, a shape that keeps reappearing, a visual composition that gives you chills—these moments are worth slowing down for. The world is not random. It's often speaking. And it usually speaks through imagery before words.

Visual cues don't have to be grand or mystical. They're often subtle. A particular symbol on someone's clothing. A phrase printed on a passing truck. A book cover that keeps showing up in different places. When you start noticing these repetitions, you begin to realize that your outer world is reflecting something back to you.

Sometimes the same symbol shows up both in your dreams and in waking life. That's not coincidence. That overlap is a sign of alignment between your inner awareness and outer experience. It means something is trying to get through to you on multiple levels. And when that happens, it's worth paying close attention.

When something repeats across both your inner and outer experience, it's not just a coincidence. It is a moment of resonance. A doorway between your consciousness and something greater. This is where symbolism becomes more than metaphor. It becomes guidance.

To work with these signs effectively, you need to start paying close attention to how they feel. Not just what they are, but what they evoke in you. Intuition is your translator. That flash of recognition, the sense that something is meaningful even if you can't explain why, is your cue to pause and listen more deeply. These moments often defy rational interpretation, and that's what makes them so powerful. They are not bound by logic. They are invitations to expand your perception.

In practical terms, this means tracking. Keep a record. Write down your dreams, even if they seem strange or fragmented. Note symbols that appear repeatedly in your day-to-day life. Pay attention to visuals that stir something in you. Over time, a personal symbolic language will begin to emerge. You will start seeing patterns, and those patterns will help you build clarity in ways no external guide ever could.

The mind is wired to look for meaning, but it's also conditioned to dismiss what it doesn't immediately understand. This is why many people overlook symbolic communication. They're waiting for something louder, more obvious, more literal. But symbols often speak in whispers. They require presence and stillness. They ask you to suspend disbelief and allow mystery to exist alongside reason.

Art is another powerful arena where symbols come alive. The music you're drawn to, the films that linger in your heart, the architecture that stuns you into silence. These are not accidental preferences. They're reflections of your inner landscape. When something visual moves you, it is telling you something about your current state, your longings, your challenges, or your next steps. You don't need to dissect it. You only need to listen with more than your mind.

There are also times when visual signs come with a jolt. You might be thinking about a life decision and suddenly see a billboard with a word that feels like an answer. Or you might feel lost, and a stranger walks past wearing a shirt that says "Keep Going." These are not always messages planted by the universe just for you. But your awareness meeting them in that moment is what creates the meaning. The dialogue is mutual. You are a co-creator in how the message lands.

This ability to receive visual signs grows as your inner stillness deepens. Meditation, time in nature, solitude, or creative practices can help open that channel. These are the spaces where the clutter of thought fades and perception sharpens. From this quiet, you begin to see what was always there, waiting for you to notice.

Importantly, you don't need to become obsessed with decoding every single detail. That would only create anxiety and confusion. The goal isn't to make life a puzzle to solve. It's to walk through it with a greater sense of awareness, grace, and presence. Trust that what needs to stand out will. Let the rest pass through.

Dreams, symbols, and visual cues are part of a larger dialogue between your inner world and the intelligence of life itself. You're not being tested. You're being invited. Every image, pattern, and symbol is a thread. Follow it not to control the future, but to deepen your trust in the invisible fabric of meaning that is always woven through the present. In the end, these signs are not separate from you. They are echoes of what you already know, returning to you in forms that bypass resistance. Your job is not to force the answers, but to remain open enough to see them when they appear.

Numbers, Names, and Timed Encounters

There are moments in life when something seems to line up too perfectly to ignore. You glance at the clock and see the same numbers again. A name keeps showing up in strange places. You run into someone at the exact time you needed their words or presence. These aren't just odd coincidences. For those who are attuned, they are precise signals that life is trying to get your attention.

Numbers are one of the most common ways these messages show up. People often talk about seeing repeating sequences—like 11:11 or 222—and wondering if they mean something. The answer is that they can. But the real power lies not in a universal meaning attached to a number, but in the personal meaning it holds for you. Numbers have frequency. They carry a vibration. That's why many ancient traditions used numerology to explore life paths, inner drives, and spiritual timing.

If a certain number keeps appearing, it's worth pausing to reflect on what you were thinking, feeling, or doing in the moment you saw it. Was your mind on a decision? Were you asking for a sign? That number may be pointing to alignment, or it may be inviting you to redirect. It might not give you a clear answer, but it will raise your awareness. And that shift in awareness is often the first step to deeper clarity.

Sometimes the number has a direct personal tie. It could be the age you were during a pivotal experience, a birthdate of someone significant, or the address where something meaningful happened. Numbers are like echoes. They repeat to wake you up, not because they have magical power on their own, but because your attention to them activates something that had been dormant. It's the noticing that creates the bridge between the physical and the spiritual.

Names are another potent form of symbolic communication. You may hear the same name multiple times in a week. It could be a name from your past, the name of someone you haven't met yet, or a name that stirs something emotional or unresolved. Pay attention when names repeat. They often emerge as reminders of what still needs your attention, or as clues that someone connected to that name carries part of the guidance you're seeking.

Even more mysterious are the names that show up in dreams or spontaneous thought. You might wake up remembering a name you haven't heard in years, or find yourself thinking about someone for no reason. And then, without planning it, you see their name on a storefront or get a message from them out of the blue. These moments are not accidental. They're part of the subtle web of signals that move around and through you. A name can serve as a symbol of something larger: a chapter, a lesson, a longing, or an unresolved thread waiting to be woven back into your life with fresh understanding.

Timed encounters are perhaps the most tangible yet most easily dismissed. Running into someone at the exact right moment can seem like nothing at all. You might say it's luck or coincidence. But if you look deeper, you might notice a pattern in these timings. Maybe you keep meeting people just when you feel most uncertain or alone. Maybe someone crosses your path the same day you were thinking of quitting or starting something big. These are the moments when the universe leans in, places someone in your path, and asks: are you paying attention? Timed encounters are not always gentle. Sometimes they're disruptive. Someone might come into your space and challenge you, press on your wounds, or reflect something back to you that you didn't want to see. That too can be a form of spiritual timing. The right person showing up at the wrong moment can be the very trigger that wakes you up.

Your environment is constantly moving, yet when something interrupts that flow in a noticeable way, it may be more than chance. An encounter at the exact second you're reaching an internal turning point carries a signature quality, as if time itself rearranged to meet you. It's not about predicting these moments, but recognizing them when they happen. Awareness is what turns a random interaction into a meaningful clue.

Some of the most powerful timed encounters happen not in conversation, but in simple presence. A stranger who sits beside you on a bench just when you're about to fall apart. A passerby wearing a message on their shirt that mirrors what you were just thinking. These seemingly minor alignments can restore a sense of connection, like someone or something is walking with you even when you feel most alone.

But this type of awareness requires you to slow down. To be available. It's easy to miss timed encounters when you're rushing through your day or lost in mental noise. Slowing down creates space for insight. It lets you catch the moment when life opens a crack and something meaningful slips through. Timing isn't just about the clock. It's about your state of presence when the moment arrives.

The more you pay attention to these signals, the more precise they become. It's not that the signs increase. It's that your inner clarity sharpens, and what was previously overlooked now feels unmistakable. Numbers stop feeling random. Names carry weight. Encounters feel scripted in a way you can't fully explain but can't deny either.

Still, this doesn't mean every repetition is a sign. Discernment matters. Seeing 1111 every day doesn't automatically mean you're on the right path. Repetition invites inquiry, not automatic belief. Ask yourself what you feel in the moment. Do you feel calm, affirmed, called to pause? Or do you feel anxious, grasping, trying to make something out of nothing? The quality of your emotion will often tell you if the moment is meaningful or if your mind is reaching for a pattern.

The mind loves patterns. But meaning isn't just in the pattern. It's in the resonance. That inner yes. That quiet pulse of knowing. When a number appears and something inside you lights up or softens, that's when you pause. When a name shows up and your body tightens or your heart aches, that's a signal too. Your internal state is part of the decoding process. The signs don't come with instructions. Your own awareness completes the message.

As you develop your inner compass, you may also begin to notice how layered these messages can be. A number might carry both a personal and symbolic meaning. A name might call you toward healing while also pointing to a next step. A chance meeting might not reveal its full purpose until weeks later. The universe doesn't always work in straight lines. Meaning often unfolds in circles.

Let yourself sit with the unknown. Not every message is meant to be fully understood right away. Some are meant to awaken a new layer of perception. Some prepare you. Others simply remind you that you're not alone, not forgotten, not moving without guidance.

Over time, as your attention becomes more finely tuned, these signs begin to weave together like threads in a larger story. You stop needing constant proof, because you begin to trust the language. You begin to live inside a more connected reality, one where nothing is wasted and even the smallest details carry significance.

The purpose of signs is not to give you all the answers. It's to remind you that answers are already unfolding, sometimes beneath the surface, sometimes within. Your task is to stay present, to stay open, and to keep listening. Numbers, names, and timings are just the starting points. The real message is always how you respond.

Chapter 5: Sign or Coincidence?

How to Test the Meaning of a Sign

Spiritual signs often arrive in moments when you're uncertain, hopeful, or quietly asking for guidance. They feel charged with meaning, almost as if something unseen is responding to your inner world. But not every striking moment is a message, and not every repetition is a signal. One of the most valuable skills you can develop on your path is the ability to test the meaning of a sign before you act on it.

Testing doesn't mean doubting. It means pausing. It means creating space between experience and interpretation. Too often, people become so eager to find meaning that they accept the first idea that comes to mind, even if it's shaped by fear, fantasy, or projection. This is where confusion begins. Learning to test a sign doesn't shut down its power. It honors it.

The first step is internal clarity. Ask yourself what question you were holding—consciously or unconsciously—when the sign appeared. Were you feeling lost? Were you seeking confirmation? Were you hoping for permission to make a decision you already sensed was right or wrong? Context is everything. A sign doesn't float in a vacuum. It appears in relation to your current emotional, mental, and spiritual state. If you don't take that into account, you risk misinterpreting the signal entirely.

The second step is presence. How did you feel the moment the sign occurred? Did something shift inside of you—your breath, your focus, your body language? Did time seem to slow down, or did you feel more grounded and awake? Genuine signs often come with a subtle but distinct change in your internal atmosphere. You may feel a sense of pause, a drop into your body, or even a wave of calm or stillness. That felt shift is important. It often marks the difference between a real sign and a random coincidence.

Once you've acknowledged both context and internal response, the next step is to ask for confirmation. This is one of the most overlooked but powerful aspects of sign interpretation. You are allowed to dialogue with the unseen. You don't have to take the first sign at face value. You can say, either aloud or internally, "If this is truly a sign meant for me, please send me a second confirmation. Let it be unmistakable. Let it reach me clearly."

This isn't a test in the skeptical sense. It's a deepening of the conversation. When a message is truly meant for you, it will often be repeated in a way that is personal, timely, and emotionally resonant. You may notice the same symbol appear in a book you randomly pick up. Or someone may say a phrase that mirrors the message you just received. Or a situation may unfold that seems to echo the same theme. The confirmation won't always be flashy. Sometimes it's subtle, but it will carry a felt sense of alignment that's hard to ignore.

The reason confirmation is so helpful is because it breaks you out of mental looping. You're no longer trying to figure out the message from a place of overthinking. Instead, you're allowing the deeper intelligence behind the sign to speak again. You are listening not just once, but twice. And in doing so, you begin to move with more trust and less doubt.

A tested sign also becomes easier to act on. When you're uncertain, you may freeze or delay. But when the message is confirmed, something inside you softens. You feel supported. You feel accompanied by something larger than your own logic. And that gives you the confidence to move forward with more clarity.

Let's now explore how signs can be misread, and how your emotional state can influence interpretation.

Misreading signs often happens when you're emotionally charged. When you're desperate for an answer, your mind becomes quick to label experiences as confirmation. In these moments, it's easy to project meaning onto things that don't hold it. A song lyric, a glance from a stranger, or a number on a receipt might feel profound not because they are, but because your nervous system is reaching for reassurance. This is why neutrality matters. The more grounded you are, the clearer your discernment becomes.

Testing also requires that you step out of urgency. Signs are not about rushing decisions. They are meant to open doors of awareness, not push you into forced action. If you feel pressed to act immediately based on something you interpreted, pause again. Urgency is often a sign of ego, not guidance. The universe speaks in timing that respects your growth. It will never push you into panic. It will call you into presence.

Another way to test a sign is to examine its alignment with your deeper truth. Ask yourself: does this message resonate with my inner values, with who I know myself to be at my core? Does it invite me to act from strength, clarity, and self-respect? Or does it feed my insecurity, inflate a fantasy, or encourage bypassing discomfort? Real signs often stretch you toward growth, but never toward self-betrayal. They may challenge you, but they will never diminish you.

Dreams, synchronicities, repeated numbers, and spontaneous events all carry the potential to act as signals. But if a "sign" is telling you something that contradicts your body's wisdom or makes you abandon your integrity, it's worth stepping back. The universe may communicate symbolically, but your soul will always be able to tell if something is off. That internal check is your compass. You don't need to rationalize a sign into being meaningful. If it is real, it will keep appearing, and it will keep pointing in the same direction.

If you're still unsure, give it time. Testing a sign doesn't require you to solve it on the spot. Sometimes you simply live with it for a few days, letting it settle into your awareness. As you go about your life, more clues may come, deepening your understanding or shifting it entirely. The passage of time can be part of the test. If the meaning holds or becomes clearer with distance, it's likely trustworthy. If it fades or starts to feel hollow, it may have been a false flag.

You can also write the sign down and journal about it without trying to analyze it too hard. Free-write what you felt when it happened. What came to mind? What was going on in your life that day? What did you feel drawn toward or away from? These intuitive reflections often reveal threads that your conscious mind might miss. Writing gives space for your inner knowing to emerge without the pressure to get it right immediately.

Most importantly, remember that testing a sign is not a rejection of the unseen. It is an honoring of it. It's choosing to listen with respect rather than anxiety. The more you practice this way of relating, the more confident you become in your interpretations. And over time, you'll find that the signs become clearer, not because they change, but because your perception sharpens.

In the end, the purpose of a sign is not just to tell you what to do, but to awaken a deeper awareness within you. The universe may use external cues to activate your internal clarity. When you test the meaning with patience and integrity, you're not just decoding the sign. You're becoming someone who no longer needs constant signs to feel guided. You're learning to trust your own inner signal. And that is the most powerful guidance of all.

The Role of Emotion and Intuition in Validation

Emotion and intuition are often the very first responses we have when something significant crosses our path. Before the mind starts analyzing or categorizing what something could mean, we feel it. There is a shift— a sensation in the body, a moment of stillness, or a pull in a certain direction. These responses are not random. They are part of a built-in system designed to help us perceive meaning beyond what is visible or explainable.

Emotion plays a vital role in the validation of spiritual signs and experiences. When a moment stirs your heart, brings tears without reason, or lights up your chest with warmth or clarity, it's not simply sentimentality. It may be your system recognizing something as true before you've had time to mentally process it. Emotional resonance is one of the strongest indicators that you are in the presence of something meaningful. It's a full-body signal that bypasses logic. You may not know exactly why something matters, but you know that it does.

This doesn't mean every emotional reaction is a confirmation. Sometimes fear, excitement, or longing can distort your interpretation. That's why emotion and intuition need to be felt fully, then observed with presence. You allow the wave of emotion to pass through you without needing to act on it immediately. Afterward, you ask: what exactly was I feeling? Was it relief, hope, clarity—or was it anxiety, pressure, or confusion? The emotion's quality can help you discern its source.

Intuition often works in tandem with emotion, but it is quieter. It doesn't shout or plead. It simply knows. Intuition might feel like a gentle certainty, a sense of direction, or an inner calm that arises even when things don't look logically sound. It isn't necessarily rooted in emotion at all—it is more of a subtle alignment. You may receive a sign that feels neutral on the surface, but your intuition still pulls you toward it, like a quiet inner magnet.

One way to begin working with intuition more consciously is to notice what your body feels like when you're aligned. When something is right, your breath deepens, your shoulders soften, and your chest may feel open. Your mind becomes quiet rather than agitated. Intuition has a grounding effect. It brings you back to yourself. In contrast, when something feels off—even if it appears perfect on the surface—you may feel unsettled, pressured, or disconnected. This is your system saying no, even when the words say yes.

Validation is about letting both emotion and intuition participate in your decision-making and your interpretation of signs. It's not enough to intellectually "figure it out." Real knowing includes the body, the heart, and the subtle cues that arise when something is energetically right. If a sign appears and your first feeling is deep resonance, followed by a calm intuitive sense of confirmation, that's usually a clear yes. If the emotion is intense but your intuition feels foggy, it might mean you need to sit with it longer before drawing conclusions.

People often dismiss their intuitive and emotional signals because they've been conditioned to trust only what they can prove. But when it comes to spiritual signs and unseen guidance, proof is rarely immediate. Your inner system becomes the proving ground. Over time, by watching how your body responds and how reality unfolds afterward, you develop a personal language of validation that is more trustworthy than anything external.

Letting emotion and intuition be part of that process doesn't mean abandoning logic. It means giving voice to the deeper intelligence within you that often sees further than the mind can. Emotion lets you feel the impact of truth. Intuition guides you toward it. When both are respected and understood, you no longer second-guess every sign. You start to recognize the ones that are meant for you by how they make you feel, and how they steady you inside.

As your sensitivity deepens, you'll begin to notice that not all signs arrive with the same emotional or intuitive weight. Some feel like a whisper, others like a thunderclap. A subtle chill on the skin, a quickening of the pulse, a sudden peace that seems to settle without explanation—these are not random sensations. They are forms of intelligence, woven through your emotional and energetic body. Honoring these nuances is key. The more you acknowledge and track these inner responses, the clearer your internal guidance system becomes.

Validation, in this context, is not just about confirming whether a sign was real. It's about confirming whether it was meant for you. Something can be symbolic or carry meaning, but it might not apply to your life or situation. Emotion and intuition help narrow the field. A symbol in a dream, for example, might be archetypal, but only certain images will evoke a personal response that lingers. That lingering is the clue. If something won't leave you alone, if it continues to stir thought, emotion, or a sense of recognition, it's worth listening.

There's also a distinction between reactive emotion and responsive emotion. Reactive emotion is immediate and often charged. It may come from past wounds, unmet needs, or fears. Responsive emotion is more grounded. It arises from presence, not from panic or projection. Learning to recognize the difference helps you avoid mistaking a personal trigger for a spiritual message. If a sign activates old fear, it's not necessarily wrong, but it requires deeper reflection. You may need to clear the emotional layer before you can truly sense the intuitive core beneath it.

The same goes for intuition. It can be clouded by desire or aversion. Wanting something too badly can generate false positives. You might interpret neutral events as confirmations simply because you're craving a certain outcome. To counter this, practice asking yourself simple, body-based questions. Does this feel like truth, or does it feel like a story I'm telling myself? Do I feel more grounded after receiving this sign, or more scattered? Is my energy expanding or contracting?

Another powerful way to validate a sign is to check how it integrates with your life after the initial moment. Does the message hold up over time? Do synchronicities continue to unfold in alignment with it? Does it inspire clarity, peace, or meaningful action? A true sign often carries a momentum of its own. It becomes part of a larger pattern. Your emotional and intuitive system keeps nudging you in the same direction, quietly and consistently.

One overlooked aspect of validation is silence. Not every sign demands an immediate response. Sometimes the most intuitive thing you can do is wait. Let the sign breathe. Let it echo. Let it find its place in the larger pattern of your experience. Often, when we stop grasping for meaning, the real meaning begins to surface. Your emotions settle. Your intuition clears. And what remains is a deeper knowing that doesn't need constant reassurance.

You are not meant to interpret signs solely from your head. The heart and the gut speak their own language. They don't use words, but they are precise. Their accuracy increases with use. The more you trust them, the stronger they become. This is how you build inner authority. Not from certainty, but from consistency. From watching, feeling, learning, and adjusting over time. Every real sign is an invitation to come home to this intelligence within.

The validation of spiritual signals is not a one-time task. It is a lifelong dialogue between your outer reality and your inner resonance. Emotion and intuition are your allies in that dialogue. They help you distinguish noise from message, fantasy from alignment, fear from truth. When you learn to trust them, you stop chasing signs and start responding to them. You begin to live in tune with the rhythm behind appearances. And in that rhythm, clarity becomes natural. Not because everything makes sense, but because everything starts to feel right.

Common Misinterpretations and False Positives

When we open ourselves to signs and spiritual signals, we enter a space where personal meaning, inner perception, and symbolic events begin to interact more vividly with daily life. But in this space, interpretation becomes both a gift and a challenge. As the volume of awareness increases, so does the potential for misreading the signals. Not all perceived signs are authentic communications from the universe. Some are projections. Some are misunderstandings. And some are simply coincidences that our mind assigns significance to because we are looking for it.

The first common misinterpretation arises from desire. When we deeply want something to be true, our mind can shape almost anything into a sign that confirms it. A person hoping to hear from a lost loved one might see their name on a billboard and take it as a message. A hopeful romantic might interpret every glance, word, or timing coincidence as destiny pointing to a relationship. The human mind seeks patterns, and when fueled by longing, it will create them. This doesn't mean those moments are empty of meaning, but it does mean we have to examine the source of our interpretation.

False positives often come from this place of emotional bias. You want an answer, so your intuition rushes to fill in the gaps. But intuition, when authentic, tends to come with a quality of calm clarity, not anxious urgency. When you're grasping for meaning, you override the deeper voice within you that might be signaling patience, caution, or even silence. One of the clearest signs that you're misinterpreting a signal is when the meaning you extract feels forced or unstable. If you have to constantly defend your interpretation, or if it brings more confusion than clarity, it's worth taking a step back.

Another common pitfall is confirmation bias. Once you've assigned meaning to a sign, your attention may become overly tuned to finding proof that supports that conclusion. You ignore conflicting signals or alternative explanations because your mind is now focused on validating the original interpretation. This creates a feedback loop where even neutral events start to look like validations. For example, if you interpret

67

a specific number as a go-ahead for a new job, you may start seeing that number everywhere. But is that truly a sign, or has your awareness simply been trained to notice it?

We also tend to confuse coincidence with spiritual significance. Synchronicity is real, but not every coincidence is a sign. Life is full of patterns and overlaps. The key is not the event itself, but the emotional and intuitive response it evokes. Two people can have the same experience, but only one of them feels a deep inner resonance. That resonance is what separates noise from message. Without that inner alignment, the outer event remains just an occurrence.

Symbol overload is another issue. As you become more familiar with signs, symbols, and meanings, it's easy to start reading into everything. A bird flying across your path, a song on the radio, a word in conversation—all of these can hold significance. But not all do. When you start interpreting every little thing, you dilute your ability to feel what truly stands out. The symbolic becomes cluttered. You no longer hear the whisper because you're drowning in noise.

A related challenge is the tendency to interpret signs from a place of fear. This often happens when people are anxious or uncertain and are looking for validation that everything will be okay. They may view neutral events as warnings or assume that the absence of a sign means something is wrong. But the absence of a sign can simply mean pause. Or rest. Or that there's nothing to interpret in that moment. Fear-based interpretation distorts the original signal. It bends the message to fit a narrative of scarcity or threat, instead of trust and openness.

Another subtle form of misinterpretation occurs when signs are filtered through the lens of superstition rather than grounded discernment. Superstition relies on rigid cause-and-effect thinking. It assumes that one symbol must always mean one specific thing, regardless of context, timing, or personal intuition. This removes the living, dynamic quality of signs and replaces it with a formula. But spiritual communication is not mechanical. It's alive. It adapts to you. A crow may mean death in one culture, but in another it may symbolize mystery, magic, or transition. The danger of superstition is that it limits the language of the universe to a fixed set of rules, stripping it of depth.

Social influence can also distort interpretation. If someone you admire insists that a specific number or dream must mean a certain thing, you might override your own inner voice to match theirs. The desire to belong, to be seen as spiritual or intuitive, can push you into interpretations that don't feel true to you. But a sign that does not speak directly to your core is not your sign. Real messages feel personal, even if they defy popular meanings or accepted interpretations. It's far more powerful to be honest with yourself than to adopt someone else's meaning just because it seems more legitimate.

Projecting meaning onto neutral events can be a form of avoidance. When something in life feels uncertain or emotionally heavy, looking for signs can become a way to escape the discomfort of not knowing. Instead of sitting with the ambiguity, the mind rushes to create meaning so it can feel a sense of control. But true spiritual communication doesn't always come when we're trying to force it. It comes when we're present enough to receive it, not when we're desperate to create it.

Another risk is over-reliance on signs for decision-making. Signs can guide and affirm, but they are not meant to replace your own responsibility, reflection, and wisdom. If every life choice is outsourced to whether a number shows up or a bird crosses your path, you lose the ability to grow in discernment and inner leadership. Signs are meant to assist your intuition, not replace it. They are companions, not commanders. Misusing them as substitutes for self-trust can stunt your development instead of deepening it.

There's also a tendency to interpret signs through personal wounds rather than clarity. When someone has experienced betrayal, abandonment, or repeated loss, they might see danger in situations that are neutral or even positive. A delay in plans may be interpreted as a punishment or warning rather than just a logistical hiccup. A disagreement with someone might feel like a sign that the relationship is doomed rather than an opportunity for growth. Trauma-colored lenses can turn even gentle signals into false alarms. That's why healing is essential if we want to interpret signs cleanly. When our nervous system is calm and our heart is open, we're much more likely to perceive things accurately.

To navigate all of this, the key is spaciousness. When a potential sign appears, don't rush to label it. Sit with it. Ask if it carries resonance or if it feels hollow. Consider whether you're grasping or receiving. Check your emotional state. If you're exhausted, anxious, or in a high state of desire, your interpretation may be skewed. But if you're grounded, clear, and willing to accept any outcome, the message has room to show itself without distortion.

False positives will happen. They're part of learning. Every interpreter of signs, no matter how seasoned, occasionally misreads the message. What matters most is the humility to acknowledge it and the willingness to refine your awareness. When you're honest with yourself, misinterpretations don't become dangerous. They become part of your growth.

True clarity doesn't feel like a high. It feels like a quiet inner alignment. That's the compass you're developing. And with practice, that compass gets stronger, more precise, and more attuned to the authentic signals life is constantly sending your way.

Chapter 6: Timing and Urgency

Delayed Signs: When Meaning Arrives Later

Some signs don't make sense until much later. They arrive unannounced, seem puzzling or insignificant, and are only understood in hindsight, when enough time and experience have passed to cast them in the proper light. These are the delayed signs, the kind that challenge our need for immediate clarity and remind us that meaning unfolds on its own timeline, not ours.

It's natural to want answers right away. When we notice something that feels symbolic or unusual—a strange encounter, a recurring image, a vivid dream—our minds instinctively try to assign meaning to it. We want to know what it means now, in this moment, especially when we're seeking guidance, direction, or reassurance. But life often speaks in incomplete messages. It gives us the beginning of a sentence, a single word, or a quiet nudge that only makes sense later, once the rest of the sentence arrives.

This delay can feel frustrating, even disorienting. It may cause doubt, or make you question whether the sign was real at all. But it's not a failure of intuition. It's a deeper part of how symbolic language operates. Some signs are seeds, not conclusions. They are meant to be carried, not solved immediately. They activate something in your awareness that slowly unfolds over time. You might forget about the sign altogether, only to look back weeks or months later and see how it fits perfectly into the larger pattern.

Delayed signs ask for a different kind of relationship with mystery. They invite you to hold uncertainty without panic, to let go of your need for instant answers. They teach you to trust the process of life, even when it doesn't explain itself. In that space of not-knowing, your perception deepens. You become more receptive, more observant, more willing to listen rather than force an interpretation.

Sometimes, a delayed sign is actually a protective mechanism. If you were to understand its full meaning too soon, you might interfere with something that needs to unfold naturally. Or you might not yet be emotionally ready to receive the truth it carries. Life has a rhythm, and it often delivers wisdom when we're ready to hold it, not a moment earlier. In that way, the delay isn't a barrier. It's grace.

One of the keys to working with delayed signs is learning to document them. When something happens that feels symbolically charged but unclear, write it down. Keep a record of repeating numbers, strange dreams, unexpected encounters, or things that feel "off." Don't try to force meaning onto them right away. Just capture the moment. You're creating a language map for your future self. What seems random now may be a missing piece in a pattern you haven't seen yet.

You'll notice that over time, delayed signs often resurface in moments of change, decision, or emotional turning points. A symbol from months ago might suddenly come to mind as you face a new path. An old dream might echo the exact scenario you're living through now. These echoes help you see that guidance has been present all along, even if you didn't recognize it at the time.

Meaning can arrive long after the moment has passed, but when it does, it lands with clarity. You feel the thread connecting past and present. You realize the sign was never random. It was simply early. And now, with the rest of the experience in place, you can finally understand what it was trying to tell you.

This is why cultivating patience is essential. Patience is not passive waiting. It's an active form of trust. It's the discipline of staying open even when the meaning isn't clear. In a world obsessed with speed, productivity, and certainty, the patience required to honor delayed signs is almost revolutionary. It requires you to surrender control, which is uncomfortable, but necessary if you want to truly work with the deeper language of life.

Holding space for a sign without prematurely defining it keeps the door open. If you rush to assign meaning, you might settle for something convenient rather than something true. But if you hold the moment with reverence, you allow your awareness to mature. Often, it is the passage of time itself that reveals the missing context. What felt vague or abstract at first becomes illuminated by experience, connection, and emotional clarity.

Your emotional state plays a major role in how and when meaning crystallizes. When you're in survival mode, anxious, or trying to force an answer, your perception narrows. You look for signs that match your fears or your current narrative, rather than what's actually being communicated. But when you're grounded, open, and emotionally clear, the same sign may present itself in a completely different light. What once triggered confusion now brings understanding. The sign didn't change. You did.

Another reason signs delay their meaning is that they often involve multiple layers. What seems like a small personal message might later unfold into something collective, relational, or even ancestral. You might first interpret an event as a coincidence, then recognize it as a personal warning, and only later realize it also mirrors a pattern in your lineage or community. This layered unfolding is part of the intelligence behind spiritual timing. Meaning is not a one-time event. It's something that can evolve and deepen as you evolve and deepen.

It's also important to recognize that sometimes the delay itself is the message. Life is showing you that you're in a cycle where answers will not come easily. Maybe you're being invited into a season of listening, rather than knowing. Maybe you're being asked to hold mystery as a form of faith. These are not comfortable places to live in, but they are often the most transformative. Not knowing can strip away the illusion of control, which leaves you more honest, more humble, and paradoxically, more connected to guidance.

This doesn't mean that every unexplainable moment is a delayed sign. Part of your discernment is knowing when to let something go and when to keep it in your awareness. If a moment continues to resonate, if it echoes in your dreams, or if it stirs something deep inside that refuses to fade, pay attention. That's a sign with a long tail. It's not done with you yet. It may be waiting for a specific alignment in your life, a new level of understanding, or a shift in emotional maturity before it fully reveals itself.

You are not meant to decode everything right away. Some messages are meant to live with you for a while, shaping your path quietly from the background. Over time, the puzzle pieces start to form an image, and what once felt uncertain becomes obvious in retrospect. That moment of realization carries a kind of sacred clarity. Not only do you understand the sign, but you also understand why it waited. You see how much had to happen in you and around you for the meaning to land.

This is the deeper rhythm of guidance. It speaks when the timing is right, not when your mind demands it. It asks you to live in alignment with time, not in opposition to it. And if you can meet that rhythm with openness and trust, you will find that even the signs that once felt silent were always speaking. They were just waiting for you to be ready to listen.

Urgent Warnings vs. Gentle Nudges

Not all signs are created equal. Some arrive softly, like a whisper in the background of your day. Others arrive with force, cutting through the noise with such intensity that they can't be ignored. Learning to tell the difference between a gentle nudge and an urgent warning is one of the most important skills on the path of spiritual discernment. It shapes how you respond, how quickly you act, and how much weight you assign to what you receive.

Gentle nudges are subtle. They often repeat over time, surfacing in quiet ways—a word that stands out in a conversation, a symbol that keeps reappearing, a light internal sensation that feels like curiosity or hesitation. These signs are not disruptive. They invite you to pay attention, to lean in with interest. They're often connected to alignment, to small course corrections that refine your path. The energy they carry is calm and open-ended. There's no pressure, only an invitation.

Many people overlook these nudges because they expect signs to be dramatic. But gentle signs are a sign of trust from the universe. You're being guided without alarm because you're already close to the right path. You're being encouraged to fine-tune your awareness, to shift something small before it becomes something big. This kind of guidance respects your ability to listen without fear. It doesn't demand. It suggests. And it usually comes with a sense of grace.

Urgent warnings, by contrast, have a very different quality. They feel disruptive. They may jolt your nervous system or stop you in your tracks. A sudden accident, an intense dream, a message that lands with overwhelming clarity or discomfort—these are not casual occurrences. They are often tied to boundaries being crossed, danger being near, or a major decision requiring immediate redirection. Urgent signs don't come often, but when they do, they tend to override your usual filters. You can feel the weight of them in your body.

These warnings often appear when you're not listening to the gentle nudges. They come as a final attempt to pull you back into alignment when more subtle cues have been ignored. That's not to say they're punishments. They're wake-up calls. They show up when something is at stake—your safety, your integrity, your spiritual timing. In some cases, they're not even for you alone, but for others you're connected to. The ripple of your decisions may impact others, and the warning comes as a collective correction.

The intensity of a sign is usually mirrored by your inner response. Pay attention to how your body reacts. A gentle nudge may come with a soft tug in your chest or a faint thought that repeats. An urgent warning, on the other hand, may create a physical jolt, a sudden coldness, a racing heart, or even tears that come without explanation. These physical reactions are not random. Your body is wired to detect danger and truth before your mind has time to rationalize. If you've ever felt your stomach drop before walking into a room, or felt uneasy for no reason and later learned why, you've already experienced this.

The mistake many people make is assuming all signs should feel intense. This leads to chasing high-stimulation experiences while ignoring the quiet, grounded forms of guidance. But a balanced spiritual life includes both. The louder messages are rare and sacred. The quieter ones are ongoing and deeply wise. One is not better than the other. They simply serve different purposes, based on the urgency of the situation and your current level of alignment.

One of the most important ways to distinguish urgency is to look at the pace and pattern of the message. Gentle nudges tend to be patient. They recur in a slow, steady rhythm, often giving you space to notice, reflect, and act when you're ready. They might show up once, then again days later, then again when you're in a similar situation. Their consistency over time builds a kind of quiet pressure, but it never overwhelms. It's like water carving stone—subtle, but powerful if received with openness.

Urgent signs, on the other hand, compress time. They feel clustered, fast, and emotionally charged. You might get three warnings in a single day, or a sudden chain of events that all point to the same red flag. There is usually a sense of timing you cannot ignore. Something inside you feels that you must act now or face a consequence. It's not about panic, but precision. There's a narrowing window in which something must be seen or changed, and the universe is raising the volume to make sure you hear it.

It's crucial, though, to discern urgency from anxiety. Urgency from the universe carries clarity, even if the message is uncomfortable. You may feel shaken, but deep down you know what to do. Anxiety, on the other hand, is often cloudy and scattered. It loops, repeats, confuses. Urgent signs point clearly in one direction, even if it's a hard one. Anxiety tells you twenty stories at once and asks you to fear all of them.

Learning to trust this distinction takes time. You build it by observing the outcomes of past decisions. Look back at times when you felt a strong inner push—what happened when you ignored it? What happened when you listened? Patterns emerge. The universe teaches you through experience, showing you again and again that it knows more than your logic does.

When you act on a gentle nudge, the reward is often peace, flow, or synchronicity. Things fall into place. You feel relieved even if the action was small. When you act on an urgent warning, the result is often protection. You avoid something that could have caused harm, delay, or deep misalignment. The relief that follows is sharper, like stepping away from a cliff just in time. Sometimes you only understand the magnitude of the warning in hindsight. But the more you listen, the less damage you have to undo.

There is also an emotional maturity that comes with respecting both types of guidance. People who only respond to loud, urgent signs tend to live in cycles of crisis. They ignore the quiet truths until they explode. On the other hand, people who are attuned to gentle nudges live with more ease. They shift course early. They don't need a storm to hear the wind change. This isn't about being better. It's about being attuned.

The world we live in often rewards speed, intensity, and drama. But spiritual awareness rewards presence. Most signs do not shout. They speak in symbols, feelings, timing, and repetition. If you become the kind of person who listens to the whisper, you won't need the scream. You'll trust yourself enough to act on that subtle pull, knowing it's real even when others don't see it.

The more you honor the language of signs, the more the universe meets you halfway. It doesn't have to chase your attention. It simply partners with it. Gentle nudges become your guidance system. Urgent warnings become rare but sacred signals. Both are there to serve you. Both speak in a language older than words, a language your soul never forgot.

How to Know When Action Is Required

One of the most difficult parts of interpreting signs is knowing when to act and when to simply observe. Not every sign calls for immediate movement. Some are confirmations, others are reminders, and a few are quiet encouragements to stay the course. But there are moments when action is necessary. Discerning those moments is a skill that deepens with awareness and trust.

The first clue that a sign requires action is the feeling of energetic urgency. This isn't the same as anxiety or fear. It feels more like a sudden shift in clarity, a moment when all the noise drops away and something stands out with undeniable importance. You may have been wondering about a decision for weeks, but then a symbol appears in a way that cuts through the doubt. It lands in your chest, not just your mind. That inner yes or no becomes impossible to ignore.

Another clue is repetition that tightens. Signs that loop with increasing frequency often do so because you're not listening. They're not trying to confuse you. They're trying to break through a filter that you may not even realize you've built. At first the nudge might be soft, like hearing a name or seeing a number. But if you resist or hesitate, the volume increases. You begin seeing the same thing everywhere. It stops being a coincidence and starts to feel personal. That escalation is often a sign that your window to respond is narrowing. When symbols intensify rather than fade, that's a cue to pause and ask what needs to be done.

Timing is another factor. The universe operates in a kind of rhythm, and sometimes a door opens for only a short time. A sudden opportunity, a chance meeting, or an intuitive pull to go somewhere specific can be the beginning of something important. If a symbol appears just before or during that opening, it's often pointing toward alignment. There's a subtle current of "now or not at all." When you catch it, things flow more easily. When you miss it, the moment might pass and not return in the same form. That's not a punishment. It's a reflection of natural cycles. Everything has a season.

Your emotional reaction can also tell you whether action is required. If a sign brings a deep inner calm, it may simply be an affirmation that you're on the right track. But if it stirs something in you, like a feeling of restlessness, excitement, or unease, it may be prompting you to change course. Emotion is a guide, not a command. It shows you what's alive inside. If a sign triggers something powerful, it's asking to be explored, not ignored.

Still, it's important not to confuse movement with meaning. Taking action does not always mean making a huge change. It can be subtle. Reaching out to someone, saying no to a situation, writing something down, or creating space for reflection may be all that's needed. The action should feel like a response, not a reaction. If you're pushing to force clarity, you're likely acting from fear. If the action feels like a release, a letting go or a stepping in with trust, you're probably aligned with what the sign is guiding you toward.

You don't need to be perfect at this. Missteps are part of learning. What matters is your willingness to engage, to experiment, and to stay curious about the messages life sends. As with any language, fluency comes from practice, not theory. Over time, you begin to recognize the tone behind each sign. Some whisper. Some warn. And some, unmistakably, call you to move.

The more you refine your awareness, the more you'll notice that the signs asking for action often arrive with a distinct clarity. It's not necessarily loud or dramatic, but it carries a kind of stillness that stands apart from your usual thoughts. The message doesn't need to be decoded. It feels self-evident. Even if the action itself feels scary or unfamiliar, the directive behind it feels simple. You know what to do, even if you're not sure how it will turn out.

One of the most misunderstood aspects of signs is the idea that you need to feel completely confident before acting. In truth, very few meaningful actions come with certainty. The presence of a sign doesn't erase doubt. What it does is shift your inner balance just enough that the desire to stay still is outweighed by the pull to move. You act not because it's easy or obvious, but because something in you recognizes that it's time.

Fear is a natural companion at this point. It rises when we step beyond what we know. But there's a difference between the fear that comes from growth and the fear that signals danger. You can learn to tell them apart

80

by the way they feel in your body. Growth-related fear is often paired with a quiet sense of rightness underneath the nerves. It doesn't paralyze. It focuses. It's like standing at the edge of a cold pool, knowing you'll be fine once you jump in. Real danger, on the other hand, feels chaotic. It clouds your thinking and disconnects you from your center. If a sign calls you to act but doing so makes your body shut down or your mind spiral, it's worth pausing to reevaluate. Action should emerge from a place of grounded presence, not desperation.

Sometimes, instead of asking "Should I act?", a more helpful question is "What would alignment look like here?" This shifts the focus away from urgency and toward clarity. Alignment means your actions match your deeper truth. If the sign is pointing toward something, and your response feels like a natural extension of your values, then it's likely the right path, even if it's uncomfortable.

There are also times when not acting is itself a form of action. Silence can be powerful. Choosing not to respond, not to chase, not to interfere can carry more spiritual intelligence than any dramatic move. The key is whether the stillness feels conscious and empowered, or passive and fear-driven. A refusal to act because you're afraid to make the wrong choice is not the same as a decision to hold space for something to unfold. One comes from avoidance. The other comes from trust.

Ultimately, the practice of knowing when to act isn't about mastering a formula. It's about deepening your relationship with your inner knowing. Signs are not commands. They're invitations. They show you possibilities, paths, and pivot points. The decision is always yours. The more attuned you become to your body, your intuition, and your emotional resonance, the more precisely you can feel when it's time to move. You stop waiting for overwhelming proof. You stop outsourcing your authority. You begin trusting your own calibration.

The real shift happens when you no longer need the signs to scream. A single, subtle nudge is enough, because you've trained yourself to feel the truth in it. You're no longer acting from fear of missing a message. You're responding from connection. That's when guidance becomes partnership. That's when your life starts to move with a different rhythm. Not rushed. Not stalled. Just ready.

Part III — Building Your Personal Framework

By now, you've begun to recognize that signs are not rare or random. They are part of a living dialogue between your inner world and the world around you. But awareness alone is not enough. To truly live in harmony with these signals, you need to build a personal framework— one that helps you interpret signs reliably, stay aligned with your own truth, and act with clarity when life presents symbolic moments.

This part of the journey is about moving from inspiration to integration. It's where abstract understanding becomes grounded practice. Without a clear framework, signs can become overwhelming or even misleading. You might find yourself chasing meaning in everything, second-guessing your instincts, or becoming dependent on external validations. That is not the purpose of this path.

The goal here is not to create a rigid system of belief, but a flexible structure that fits your own rhythm, experiences, and inner compass. Your framework should help you discern which signals are worth following, which ones require patience, and which are just noise. It should guide you without confining you.

In the chapters ahead, we'll explore how to test the accuracy of your interpretations, how to distinguish emotional projections from true intuitive guidance, and how to build trust in your internal process. We'll also address the common pitfalls that can lead people to misread or misuse signs, and how to avoid becoming overly reliant on them.

This is where the deeper work happens. It's not just about decoding external messages anymore. It's about strengthening the foundation inside you so that when signs appear, you're not just seeing them— you're ready to meet them with presence, discernment, and purpose.

This is where signs become a language you can speak fluently. Where intuition becomes a skill, not a mystery. And where guidance becomes something you no longer search for, but something you live from.

Chapter 7: Learning Your Inner Language

The Way Your Body Signals Truth

Your body knows things before your mind does. It is a finely tuned instrument that constantly picks up on information—subtle cues, emotional undercurrents, energy shifts—and processes it faster than your rational thinking ever could. When something is true for you, your body responds. And when something is off, it also lets you know.

Many people have been taught to ignore these physical responses in favor of logic and external validation. We're trained to prioritize what sounds reasonable, what others agree with, or what can be explained. But the body does not lie. It tells the truth even when we're not ready to hear it. Learning to listen to its signals is one of the most powerful tools in building a reliable spiritual framework.

There are physical sensations that often accompany alignment. A sense of ease. A deep breath you didn't know you were holding. Goosebumps. A lightness in your chest. Tingling in your spine. These reactions aren't random. They are physiological affirmations—your body's way of saying, "Yes, this is right for you."

Conversely, when something is wrong, even if it appears logical on the surface, the body contracts. You might feel tension in your stomach, tightness in your jaw, or restlessness in your limbs. Your breathing may become shallow, or your heart might race. These are not just stress responses. Often, they are warning signs, early alerts that something doesn't sit right with your deeper self.

Of course, not every bodily reaction is spiritual. Sometimes discomfort comes from fear, trauma, or old conditioning. That's why discernment is key. You need to become familiar with your body's baseline and learn how your truth feels versus your fear. This requires consistent self-inquiry, patience, and the willingness to observe yourself without judgment.

Start by paying attention in everyday moments. Notice how your body responds to certain people, decisions, or environments. When you say yes to something, does your body relax or tense? When you think about a path you want to follow, do you feel energized or drained? These subtle sensations are your guidance system. They are not irrational. They are instinctive.

The body stores memory. It remembers what safety feels like. It also remembers betrayal, manipulation, and the ache of ignoring your own needs. That's why it reacts faster than the mind, which often tries to rationalize or explain away discomfort. The body doesn't debate. It simply reacts. And when you've built a relationship with its signals, you can begin to trust that reaction as a valid form of truth.

Many spiritual traditions, from Indigenous practices to somatic therapies, have long recognized the body as a sacred vessel of wisdom. They teach that intuition is not something abstract, but something physical—an embodied knowing that must be felt, not just thought. When your body and intuition work together, they create a stable internal compass that can help you navigate life with clarity.

This is particularly helpful when interpreting signs. You may see something symbolic, but unless your body resonates with it, you might be projecting meaning that isn't really there. On the other hand, a seemingly small moment can take on deep significance if it causes a clear, physical response in you. That's a sign worth paying attention to.

What makes the body so trustworthy in these moments is that it responds in real time. It doesn't filter through ego, social approval, or overanalysis. Its message is immediate, clean, and honest. You don't need to explain it to others or even to yourself. You only need to feel it and respect what it tells you.

One of the most effective ways to develop trust in your body's signals is to slow down enough to notice them. This doesn't require elaborate rituals or spiritual training. It starts with presence. With paying attention when something feels slightly off or unusually clear. With giving yourself a few quiet moments before reacting. In those moments, you can detect the smallest inner shifts—your breath catching, a sudden warmth in your chest, a pull in your gut. These are not distractions. They are data. They are the language your body uses to speak its truth.

To separate truth from emotional reactivity, it helps to distinguish between immediate instinct and conditioned response. Fear-based reactions often feel sharp, chaotic, or sudden, like a jolt. They are tied to past experiences and protective patterns. They speak loudly and demand urgent action. Truth, on the other hand, tends to emerge as a steady pulse. It may feel quiet, but it is grounded. It doesn't rush or push. It simply waits to be acknowledged. If you can sit with a sensation long enough, the difference between panic and inner knowing becomes clearer.

This also means learning how to sit with discomfort. Sometimes the truth your body signals isn't comfortable or convenient. It might point you away from something you thought you wanted, or toward a difficult decision. Your body may show you where you've been betraying yourself, even subtly. When this happens, the impulse might be to numb, deny, or distract. But the power lies in staying present with the signal. Breathing into it. Asking, without judgment, "What are you trying to show me?"

Over time, a map begins to form. You start to notice patterns in your body's responses. Maybe your chest tightens when you say yes out of obligation. Maybe your hands tingle when you're on the right path. These are personal truths, not universal formulas. Your body's signals are unique to you. No book, teacher, or guide can interpret them better than you can once you're attuned to them. The more you honor these cues, the more precise they become.

There's also a sacredness in reclaiming your body as a vessel of truth, especially in a world that constantly tries to pull you outside of yourself. Marketing, media, and even well-meaning advice often encourage you to override your inner signals. You're told to "push through," "power past," or "follow the plan." But spiritual alignment doesn't come from ignoring your body. It comes from making it your ally.

In relationships, this awareness becomes even more valuable. You might find that someone's words seem kind, but your stomach clenches every time they speak. Or that a situation looks promising on paper, but your body feels drained just thinking about it. These are not coincidences. Your body is scanning not just words, but energy, tone, intention. It's reading between the lines, even when your conscious mind hasn't caught up.

In moments of deep alignment, the body often enters a state of coherence. Your heart rate steadies. Your breath deepens. You may feel as if time slows, as if your entire being is in agreement. These experiences are unmistakable. They create a memory you can return to, a reference point that reminds you of what truth feels like. The more often you feel this coherence, the more clearly you can detect when it's missing.

At its core, the body is not separate from your spiritual path. It is one of its most reliable messengers. It is the meeting point where the seen and unseen converge. Where the soul whispers and the physical form responds. When you begin to live from this place, truth is no longer something you chase or question. It becomes something you feel, something you recognize, and something you trust—fully, deeply, and without hesitation.

Interpreting Emotional Charges as Guidance

Emotions are often misunderstood. They are labeled as irrational, inconvenient, or something to be "managed." But in truth, emotions carry intelligence. They are one of the most precise internal compasses you have. When an emotional charge surfaces—especially one that feels intense, disproportionate, or persistent—it is rarely random. It often points to something deeper, something that requires attention, acknowledgment, or action.

An emotional charge is more than a passing feeling. It has a weight to it. It grabs your attention. It might come in the form of irritation when someone makes a casual comment. It might show up as grief when watching a movie, even though the story has no connection to your life. It might emerge as sudden anger, sadness, or even elation without a clear trigger. These spikes are not mistakes. They are clues. They highlight areas where your deeper self is speaking.

When you experience a strong emotional reaction, the first instinct might be to suppress it or explain it away. You may try to stay "rational" or unaffected. But the truth is that emotional charges often appear precisely because something within you is being activated. That activation can come from a buried wound, a suppressed truth, an unmet need, or a moment of deep alignment. Instead of dismissing the emotion, you can learn to investigate it.

The process begins by noticing without judgment. Label the feeling if you can. Is it fear, resentment, longing, joy, shame? Once it's named, go further. Ask: what about this moment made that feeling surge forward? What belief did it bump into? What expectation was triggered? Often, emotional charges arise when there's a mismatch between your internal truth and your external experience.

For example, a job opportunity might look perfect on the surface, but you feel a sense of dread every time you imagine accepting it. That dread might be telling you something isn't aligned. Or perhaps you feel an unshakable anger after a simple disagreement. That anger might not be about the present moment at all—it could be echoing a deeper pattern of not being heard, seen, or respected in your life. In both cases, the emotion is offering you information. It is trying to guide you back to awareness.

This doesn't mean that every emotion is a signal to act immediately. Sometimes an emotional charge is asking for reflection, not reaction. What matters is that you don't ignore it. Let it speak. Let it unravel. Emotional guidance doesn't always provide answers instantly. It may take time, space, and a willingness to feel uncomfortable truths. But the more you pay attention, the more you begin to see the wisdom behind each wave.

Some emotional charges are clear and unmistakable. A deep sense of peace in someone's presence. A sharp resistance toward a certain environment. Others are subtler. A vague restlessness. A sense that something feels "off." These too are messages, even if they don't shout. Learning to interpret emotional guidance means learning to trust your body's subtle reactions as much as its loud ones. You become a listener, not just to the content of your thoughts, but to the energy beneath them. True emotional clarity often arrives when you sit with the feeling instead of trying to fix it. When you stop asking, "How do I get rid of this?" and start asking, "What is this here to show me?" In that shift, emotion transforms from a problem to a pathway. It becomes a doorway into greater alignment, a signal pointing toward truth, growth, and deeper self-connection.

What often surprises people is that emotional charges don't always show up around obviously significant situations. Sometimes, the most revealing signals come from small moments. A casual conversation, a piece of music, an image that stirs something deep in you. These reactions are not accidental. They are mirrors. When something ordinary provokes an extraordinary emotional response, it's because your inner world recognizes something unspoken, something unresolved, or something meaningful.

Paying attention to emotional guidance also means recognizing the physical sensations that accompany it. The body speaks in its own language. A tight chest, a flutter in the stomach, a wave of warmth, a sudden chill—these physical cues often parallel emotional truths. They act as somatic signals that point to what the conscious mind might not yet be able to articulate. When you feel an emotional charge, ask where it lands in your body. That awareness anchors the experience and allows for more honest interpretation.

Learning to interpret emotional charges as guidance also involves noticing patterns over time. If the same emotional spike keeps appearing in certain situations or with certain people, there is likely a deeper lesson waiting to be revealed. Repetition is not random. It's often the soul's way of drawing your attention to something that you've tried to avoid or something that you're ready to transform.

One of the most powerful shifts you can make is moving from resistance to curiosity. Instead of labeling emotions as good or bad, welcome them as messages. Curiosity opens the door to understanding. When you stop fighting what you feel and start listening to it, you invite a deeper intelligence to emerge. The emotional charge then becomes a signal, not a disruption. You start to ask different questions. What truth am I not seeing? What need am I ignoring? What part of me is asking to be acknowledged?

This approach does not mean dramatizing every feeling or overanalyzing every fluctuation. Discernment is key. Not every emotional flicker requires deep inquiry. But when something lingers, when a feeling refuses to pass, that's when you pause. That's when you turn inward. Often, beneath that emotional charge lies a boundary that has been crossed, a truth that hasn't been voiced, or a calling that has been neglected. The charge is the body's way of demanding attention to something that matters.

As you strengthen this practice, you begin to trust your emotional intelligence more deeply. You stop needing external validation for every choice. You feel when something is right, not because it's logical or popular, but because your inner system resonates with it. This is emotional guidance at its purest. It is not impulsive. It is not reactive. It is intuitive knowing carried through the current of your emotions.

This deeper trust also allows you to stay grounded when emotions become intense. You no longer fear them. You no longer see them as something to overcome. Instead, you meet them like an old friend who knows you well, even when they speak hard truths. Emotional charges then stop being threats and start being thresholds. They take you to the edge of your current perception and invite you to step into something wider, clearer, and more honest.

In the end, interpreting emotional charges is not about mastering your emotions. It's about partnering with them. Letting them guide you not into chaos, but into coherence. When you embrace emotion as a messenger of the soul, you stop chasing clarity from the outside. You learn to feel your way forward, guided by the wisdom already alive within you.

Calibrating to Your Own 'Yes' and 'No' Responses

One of the most empowering skills you can develop in your spiritual life is the ability to recognize your own internal "yes" and "no." These signals are not abstract or symbolic in the way dreams or synchronicities might be. They are direct responses from your inner guidance system. Learning to calibrate to them helps you make aligned decisions, avoid unnecessary confusion, and trust yourself in ways that run deeper than thought.

This calibration begins with awareness. Everyone has a unique internal language. For some, a "yes" might feel like a warmth in the chest, a lightness in the stomach, or a quiet sense of peace. For others, it may come as a clear surge of energy, like something in the body gently moving forward. A "no," by contrast, might feel like tension, pressure in the head, or a sense of withdrawal. Sometimes it's as simple as the sensation of shrinking, pulling back, or tightening. These cues are not always loud or dramatic. In fact, they are often subtle at first, especially if you've spent years overriding them.

Many people have been taught to ignore their internal signals. Social conditioning trains us to seek approval, follow logic, and prioritize external opinions over inner knowing. Over time, this can dull your ability to hear yourself clearly. You may second-guess a clear "no" because it doesn't make sense on paper. You may hesitate to follow a "yes" because it feels inconvenient or unfamiliar. Rebuilding that connection takes time, but it's entirely possible.

A powerful way to begin the process is by remembering how your body naturally reacts when you feel safe, seen, or inspired. Revisit moments when you felt a strong internal "yes"—whether it was about a relationship, a decision, or a creative idea. What did it feel like? Where did you feel it? Did your breathing shift? Did your posture change? The body doesn't lie. It responds to alignment with unmistakable clarity, even when the mind is unsure.

Once you can identify your physical and emotional "yes," you can begin to contrast it with the experience of a "no." Recall times when you said yes to something that turned out to be misaligned. How did your body respond before you moved forward? Were there hesitations you ignored? Did something feel off, even if you couldn't explain it? These reflections are not for blame, but for pattern recognition. The more honestly you observe yourself, the clearer your inner compass becomes. As you practice, start small. Tune in during low-stakes decisions. What do you want to eat? Where do you want to go today? Whom do you want to call or avoid? Use these moments to feel the internal movement of yes or no without judgment. You are not trying to be right. You are learning to listen. Calibration isn't about getting everything perfect. It's about building intimacy with your own truth.

Eventually, this inner sensitivity becomes a reliable filter through which you can sense what resonates and what repels. It guides you not just in practical decisions, but in deeper spiritual discernment. What path feels life-giving? What relationship feels life-draining? Where do you feel your soul lean in? Where does it pull away?

With time, those bodily signals become more nuanced. A "yes" doesn't always come with a full-body rush of certainty. Sometimes it's a quiet clarity that remains steady no matter how many fears or doubts try to drown it out. And a "no" might not be dramatic or emotional. It might show up as fatigue, indifference, or a simple lack of energy when thinking about the option. Learning to recognize these subtler layers allows you to make more refined distinctions and avoid misinterpreting emotional noise as inner truth.

This calibration is also influenced by the nervous system. When you're in a dysregulated state—tired, overwhelmed, or anxious—your signals can become harder to read. A trauma-activated "no" can feel like a full-body shutdown even when something is actually safe. And sometimes what feels like a "yes" is just a relief from pressure or fear, not true alignment. That's why it's essential to practice checking in when you're grounded. Make important decisions from a state of inner calm, not reaction. This doesn't mean waiting for perfect peace, but learning to tell the difference between intuition and urgency.

The body often speaks in layers. There may be a part of you that feels drawn toward something, while another part resists. In these moments, both "yes" and "no" can appear simultaneously, and it becomes important to explore which one feels deeper, more rooted. Is the resistance protective or insightful? Is the pull genuine or compensatory? These are the kinds of questions that deepen your relationship with your inner system. You're not just chasing answers. You're listening with presence and curiosity.

Practicing this kind of discernment builds emotional maturity. It makes you less dependent on external validation because you've developed your own sensing mechanism. It also cultivates a sense of safety within yourself. You begin to trust that you won't abandon your knowing to please others or avoid discomfort. That trust strengthens your connection to your purpose, your relationships, and your ability to navigate life with integrity.

Calibration is not static. It evolves with you. As your self-awareness grows, your "yes" and "no" become more precise. What once felt right may no longer resonate, and that shift is part of your spiritual growth. There's no failure in outgrowing past decisions or changing direction. That's what happens when you're genuinely listening. You allow life to speak through you, and you respond in real time.

This process also supports spiritual communication. When you're attuned to your own inner responses, external signs become clearer. You're not grasping for meaning or projecting fantasies onto the world. You're meeting the symbols and patterns with a grounded awareness of how they feel in your body and heart. You know when something feels alive, expansive, and real—and when it doesn't.

Eventually, you'll reach a place where you no longer question whether you can trust yourself. You'll still feel doubt at times, but it won't stop you from listening. You'll move with more clarity, speak with more honesty, and act with more peace. Not because you've figured everything out, but because you've finally made a home inside your own signal system. That's the true power of calibration. It's not about having all the answers. It's about knowing which direction your soul is pointing you toward, and having the courage to follow it.

Chapter 8: Creating Your Personal Signs Glossary

Tracking and Categorizing Your Past Signs

Many of the signs that shape your path aren't immediately understood in the moment. Some pass unnoticed, while others leave a deep impression that lingers without clarity. Only later do they seem to reveal their meaning, often after the consequences have unfolded. This is why looking back matters. Reflection turns random experiences into a coherent map. By tracing the signals that have shown up before, you begin to recognize the language the universe uses to speak to you personally.

Start with moments that altered your course. Think about situations where something unexpected seemed to redirect your plans or challenge your assumptions. Ask yourself: was there any kind of sign before that shift happened? Did anything stand out—a repeated phrase, a strange dream, a surge of emotion, a physical sensation, or even a subtle knowing that you ignored? These are the raw materials of your inner archive, and they often reveal more on the second or third review than they did when first experienced.

Keeping track of past signs is not about romanticizing every coincidence. It's about becoming a better listener. It helps to choose a method of recording that fits naturally into your life. For some, that might be a dedicated notebook where signs, dreams, patterns, and intuitive hits are written down. For others, it might be a digital journal, a voice memo, or even a section in your planner. The tool doesn't matter. What matters is the act of documenting what feels out of the ordinary or charged with deeper meaning.

Over time, this creates a pattern language that is entirely unique to you. You'll begin to notice certain symbols or scenarios that keep showing up. Maybe owls appear every time you're about to make a major decision. Or certain number sequences tend to arise when you're doubting yourself. Perhaps your body always gets a sudden chill before something unexpected happens. What matters is that you're not relying on someone else's dictionary of signs. You're building your own. That's how your relationship with spiritual guidance becomes real and trustworthy.

To do this effectively, clarity is essential. When documenting a potential sign or intuitive moment, include what was happening at the time. Where were you? What were you thinking about or struggling with? How did the experience make you feel in your body and emotions? What decision or change occurred soon afterward? These connections often reveal themselves more clearly after some distance, so being specific in your notes helps future you decode the full picture.

Sometimes a sign will only make sense months or even years later. You may look back and realize that a conversation you dismissed actually contained the insight you needed, or that a conflict pointed you toward the lesson you were meant to learn. These realizations are rarely obvious when you're in the middle of things. That's why regular reflection is part of the process. Even five or ten minutes once a week to revisit old entries can help you sharpen your awareness and see what you once missed.

As you track your personal signs, resist the urge to rush into conclusions. Not every emotional moment or strange occurrence holds deep spiritual meaning. Some are just life unfolding. Others, however, repeat with such precision or intensity that they ask for your attention. That's where categorizing becomes useful—not to label things rigidly, but to start grouping similar signals so you can more easily identify their frequency and function in your life.

Let's now explore how to do that intuitively and without overcomplication.

You can begin categorizing your signs by loosely grouping them into themes based on how they tend to show up. For instance, some signs arrive through sensory impressions: sights, sounds, smells, or bodily sensations. Others might come in the form of emotional surges, recurring thoughts, vivid dreams, or external synchronicities. By grouping signs this way, you begin to understand how your system of communication is wired. One person might feel everything in their chest before a significant event, while another might get symbolic messages through overheard conversations or images that appear multiple times across unrelated settings. These patterns are not random; they reflect your personal interface with guidance.

It's important to treat these categories not as fixed truths, but as living tools. You are not building a rigid system. You are listening in a more refined way. Over time, you may find that a certain category of signs tends to carry a particular kind of message. For example, physical sensations might often relate to danger or urgency. Dreams might bring clarity about something still unconscious. Numbers or symbols could indicate alignment or misalignment. Naming these associations for yourself helps create a working vocabulary between you and the intelligence that guides you.

One useful method is to reflect on moments when you followed a sign and it led to a beneficial outcome. Trace what kind of sign it was, what it pointed you toward, and how you responded. Then do the same for a time when you ignored a sign or misread it. What do those two experiences have in common? Were there signs you dismissed that, in hindsight, were unmistakably trying to get your attention? This isn't to create guilt or regret. It's about learning your way of listening, your blind spots, and your strengths.

Once you've built this personal archive and its categories, it becomes easier to assess new signs as they come. You begin to recognize familiar energetic signatures. A twinge in your gut might now immediately register as a red flag because of how often it's coincided with misaligned decisions in the past. Or you might give more weight to a symbol you used to overlook, now that you've seen it reliably mark the arrival of new opportunities. Your process becomes less about guesswork and more about attunement. The language of signs is not vague when you learn to recognize its grammar.

Sometimes, though, signs evolve. Just as you grow and change, so too may the way your inner or outer world sends you guidance. You may go through seasons where your dreams become less clear, while your intuition sharpens through bodily cues. Or you might find that synchronicities begin arriving through people and conversations rather than symbols or images. This is natural. Your relationship with spiritual signaling is dynamic, not fixed. That's why tracking must remain an active, ongoing practice rather than a one-time effort.

It's also helpful to revisit your notes from a place of curiosity rather than analysis. Ask yourself what these signs are trying to teach you about trust, fear, timing, and choice. Often, patterns point not just to events, but to inner themes that are unfolding over time. You may notice, for example, that signs tend to appear more strongly when you are resisting a necessary change, or that they grow quieter when you are fully in flow. These subtle differences carry deep messages. They invite you not just to interpret signs, but to align your life with their rhythm.

Ultimately, the practice of tracking and categorizing your past signs is a way to reclaim your spiritual memory. It grounds the abstract into something tangible. It moves you from confusion to clarity, from passive hope to active participation. When you know how signs have spoken to you before, you can better understand what they are saying now. And when new signs arise, you are no longer scrambling to decode them. You're listening from experience, not just intuition. That's when guidance becomes not just occasional, but reliable. And that's when your path becomes not just guided, but consciously chosen.

Recognizing Unique Symbols That Speak to You

Some signs are universal. A sudden storm during a funeral, a crow cawing at dusk, or a series of repeating numbers often carry collective meaning. But beyond these, there exists a personal language of symbols that is yours alone. These symbols do not come from books or traditions. They arise from your own lived experience. And when they appear, they often bypass logic and speak directly to your inner knowing.

To recognize these symbols, you must begin by noticing the things that seem to follow you. Not in a fearful sense, but with a curious and persistent presence. Perhaps there is a certain animal that always shows up during key transitions in your life. Maybe you have a recurring dream image that lingers even when you wake. It could be a phrase that strangers keep saying to you. A place that shows up in films, conversations, or memories. These are not accidents. They are patterns, and in those patterns is a hidden language designed just for you.

The first key to understanding your personal symbols is emotional resonance. When a symbol touches you, you feel something shift inside. You may not know what it means at first, but its appearance creates a pause. It catches your breath or causes you to look twice. That small interruption in your usual rhythm is a clue. It says, "Pay attention here." It invites you to ask, "What is this trying to tell me?"

This process becomes more intuitive over time. You begin to catalog these personal symbols not by writing long explanations, but by sensing how they move you. You remember the day you saw a fox on the side of the road just before making a difficult choice. You recall the specific song that played every time you were on the verge of ending a toxic relationship. These aren't just coincidences. They are your symbols speaking in ways that no external authority can define.

What makes this symbolic language powerful is its intimacy. Unlike general meanings assigned in dream dictionaries or spiritual manuals, your symbols are shaped by your own emotional history. A rose may be a symbol of love for one person, and for another, a reminder of grief. A broken clock might signify wasted time to one person, and divine timing to someone else. The meaning is not fixed. It lives inside your relationship to it.

One effective way to start tracking these symbols is to reflect on the moments in your life that felt charged. Turning points. Big decisions. Shocking surprises. Heartfelt prayers. Go back to those memories and ask what surrounded them. Were there objects, animals, images, words, or sounds that stood out? You might find that certain elements repeat across unrelated situations. That is not random. That is recognition.

When a symbol continues to appear in your life, its meaning often deepens. What it meant five years ago may not be what it means today. That's because your consciousness has evolved, and so your dialogue with that symbol becomes more refined. It's like learning to speak with someone over time. You begin with simple exchanges. Then, slowly, you understand the nuances, the tone, the pauses between the words. Your symbols become like old friends who say more with a glance than others can with a speech.

This relationship with symbols is sacred. It teaches you that you are not just reading the world but in constant conversation with it. And when you begin to trust these private messages, even the mundane becomes meaningful. A leaf stuck to your windshield. A word that keeps showing up in books. A moment of déjà vu. They are all potential doors, waiting to be opened.

When you start to pay attention to your recurring personal symbols, you begin to see a kind of dialogue forming between you and the unseen. The universe no longer feels like a distant, abstract force. It becomes intimate, personal, and alive with responsiveness. This recognition can change the way you make decisions, relate to people, or even interpret challenges. The symbols do not necessarily make life easier, but they add a layer of clarity and meaning that reshapes your understanding of events.

Many people find that once they acknowledge a personal symbol, its presence becomes even more consistent. For example, someone might realize that owls tend to appear during periods of transition or deep introspection. After this recognition, the appearance of an owl—

whether in real life, a dream, or an image—can act as a gentle confirmation to pause and reflect rather than push forward.

It's important to trust your own instinct about what a symbol means for you. External interpretations can sometimes help clarify or expand your perspective, but they should never override your inner knowing. If the world around you begins to light up with signs, and certain images or experiences stir something deep within, it's worth listening closely. That stirring, that energetic resonance, is the language of symbols at work.

Some symbols will speak softly while others shout. The quiet ones may show up in the background, nudging you without demanding attention. These might be numbers you only see when your heart is conflicted, or a melody that plays when you're questioning a decision. Louder symbols may interrupt your routine, catching you off guard or pushing you to act. The difference is not in importance, but in intensity and immediacy. Both are part of your unique system of communication.

To deepen your relationship with personal symbols, it helps to build a record. When you experience something that feels significant, write it down. Note how you felt, what was happening around you, and what seemed to follow. Over time, patterns will emerge. You may see that a particular phrase always shows up when you're out of alignment, or that certain imagery arrives right before breakthrough moments. These patterns are like a private dictionary of spiritual communication that only you can create.

This isn't about superstition. It's about awareness. Your life has a rhythm, and the universe mirrors that rhythm with echoes, hints, and reflections. When you pay attention, your perception sharpens. You begin to move in sync with something greater than logic. Life becomes more fluid, more responsive, and strangely cooperative.

And when doubts arise—and they will—it's okay. You are not meant to interpret everything perfectly or turn your life into a decoding exercise. The point is not to obsess, but to stay open. If a symbol keeps showing up, ask why. If one disappears, trust that you've received what you needed from it. Keep your curiosity alive, and remember that this language is not meant to control you, but to accompany you.

Ultimately, recognizing the symbols that speak to you is an act of honoring your own path. It means saying yes to a world that is rich with meaning and willing to meet you in unexpected ways. You are not just a receiver of signs, but a participant in the conversation. The more you trust that, the more fluent you become in reading the universe as it writes its messages just for you.

How to Document Your Sign Language System

You already receive signs. You've seen the numbers repeating, heard the songs that seem to echo your thoughts, noticed the timing of unexpected encounters or sudden feelings. What you may not yet have done is to turn this scattered awareness into a clear, grounded system that helps you navigate your life with greater trust and clarity. Documenting your personal sign language system is not about capturing every moment or cataloging spiritual events like data. It is about building a meaningful structure that reflects your unique relationship with the unseen patterns shaping your life.

The act of documentation deepens awareness. When you write something down, you give it form. You claim it. You bring it out of the realm of fleeting intuition and place it into your lived reality. This process isn't about proving anything to anyone else. It's about creating a map you can refer to when things become murky, when doubt creeps in, or when you need to remember that the guidance never really stopped—it just got quiet.

You don't need a complicated tool or app to begin. A simple notebook, a dedicated section in your journal, or even a document on your phone will work. What matters is that it feels accessible and personal to you. The key is consistency, not perfection. Each time something stands out—a number sequence, a dream, an animal, a phrase someone repeats without knowing why—make note of it. Jot down what happened, when it occurred, what you were thinking or feeling, and what followed afterward.

What you're building over time is not just a list of events, but a personal language guide. You'll start to see connections you didn't notice at first. Maybe you realize that every time you see a hawk, clarity follows within twenty-four hours. Maybe certain songs only appear when you're on the edge of a big decision. Or maybe the name of a place keeps popping up, and later you find out it's related to an opportunity or a healing moment. These are not coincidences to dismiss. They are markers, indicators, reminders that there is something deeper at play.

As your documentation grows, certain themes will begin to repeat. Symbols will return. Some may evolve in meaning over time, while others remain consistent anchors. Writing them down helps you stay connected to their original emotional impact, which is often the most accurate indicator of their relevance. Even when you don't fully understand what a sign means at the moment, preserving it gives you the opportunity to revisit it later with new insight. What once felt random can later be revealed as essential.

This practice can also sharpen your discernment. Not everything unusual is a sign, and not every emotional wave carries a message. When you're documenting, you're not just recording what stands out—you're learning how to filter. You'll begin to notice which experiences feel energetically charged and which are more neutral or simply curious. Over time, this builds trust in your inner guidance. You no longer need to overthink every detail because you're developing an intuitive fluency. The more familiar you become with your own patterns, the easier it is to tell the difference between noise and signal.

Let this be a practice of intimacy, not analysis. You're not assembling evidence to argue for the existence of signs. You're honoring the way your life already speaks to you, quietly and precisely, in a language that only you were meant to understand.

When you begin treating your signs as part of an evolving dialogue rather than isolated events, something changes. The space between you and the unseen narrows. You are no longer just a receiver, but also a participant. This shift in posture invites a different quality of communication, one that is more reciprocal, more attuned. And that is where the real clarity begins.

It's not about collecting signs for the sake of fascination. It's about cultivating a relationship with your own inner knowing. The more consistently you engage with the signs that come your way, the more naturally your system starts to unfold. Patterns reveal themselves with less effort. Interpretations become cleaner. You recognize, more quickly, when something is relevant and when it's not. You're no longer swimming in ambiguity. Instead, you begin to develop a sense of grounded confidence in what is being shown to you.

You may notice certain periods of your life become denser with symbolic communication, while others go quiet. This is normal. You're not doing anything wrong when the signs seem to disappear. Often, the guidance steps back to allow you to integrate what you've already received. The space between signs is part of the system too. Recording this ebb and flow is just as valuable as noting what shows up. Silence can have meaning. Stillness can carry insight.

Over time, you'll find your log evolves. It becomes more than a list—it becomes a language key. You might develop categories, not to limit meaning, but to reflect how signs tend to show up for you. For example, maybe animals often appear as emotional confirmations, while numbers bring intellectual clarity. Maybe song lyrics show up when your heart needs soothing, and dreams are reserved for the messages your conscious mind resists. These relationships are personal. No book or teacher can define them for you better than your lived experience can.

You are not expected to get every interpretation right. Part of documenting your sign language system is allowing space for ambiguity. You're not creating a fixed rulebook. You're crafting a flexible, living structure that adjusts as your awareness deepens. There is no shame in misreading a sign. In fact, the process of reviewing older entries with fresh eyes often reveals how much you've grown in your discernment. What once felt confusing may later strike you with obvious clarity. This isn't failure. It's evolution.

Trust will grow in proportion to your consistency. The simple act of noting your experiences, without rushing to analyze or draw conclusions, creates a stabilizing effect. It shows your subconscious that these messages matter, that your attention is not fleeting. It sends a signal that you are willing to engage, and in response, your intuitive sensitivity begins to sharpen. You start catching things in real time, not just in hindsight. What was once a whisper now feels like a clear nudge.

Above all, remember that this practice is yours. There is no right way to record, categorize, or reflect. Some people thrive with structured journals. Others keep their documentation in voice notes or sketches or quiet reflections during a walk. What matters most is the presence you bring. When you meet your signs with openness, honesty, and curiosity, you create a field where more meaning can be revealed.

You are building a bridge between the visible and invisible. You are learning to read the sacred language of your life. And as you continue to document with care, your map will take shape—not to tell you what to believe, but to remind you what you already know.

Chapter 9: Discernment and Decision-Making

When to Act and When to Wait

One of the most challenging aspects of working with signs is not identifying them, but knowing what to do after they arrive. The moment of recognition often brings a spark of clarity or emotion, but the path forward isn't always immediate. Some signs seem to call for direct action. Others feel like gentle suggestions or subtle nudges that ask you to pause, reflect, or simply observe. And learning to discern the difference can mean the difference between moving in flow and acting in haste.

The modern world conditions us to respond quickly. Everything moves fast. Notifications, deadlines, decisions. We're praised for being decisive and warned against waiting too long. But spiritual communication does not operate on the same timeline. Signs are often delivered with perfect timing, but that timing doesn't always align with the external pace of your life. This mismatch can create inner tension. You may feel a strong urge to respond, while another part of you feels hesitant. You may second-guess yourself, fearing that hesitation means missing out. But not every sign demands immediate movement. Some are simply there to prepare you.

One key to discerning whether it's time to act or time to wait lies in the emotional charge that accompanies the sign. If the message lands with panic, pressure, or desperation, it's likely being filtered through fear rather than true guidance. Urgency rooted in fear rarely leads to aligned action. On the other hand, if a sign comes with a calm inner knowing, even if it involves risk or uncertainty, that's often a green light. Inner stillness, even in the face of big decisions, is a powerful indicator of alignment.

Your body can offer additional clues. When a sign calls you to act, there's often a sense of inner expansion. The energy feels open. There might be a wave of excitement or a sense that something just clicked into place. Conversely, when it's not time to move yet, you may feel tension, resistance, or heaviness, even if the sign itself was positive. That tension is not always a signal to override, but rather an invitation to slow down and listen deeper.

There are times when a sign is part of a larger sequence. It may not make complete sense on its own because it's meant to be one piece of a longer conversation. Acting too quickly on a partial message can lead to missteps, even if the sign itself was accurate. In these cases, your role is to stay aware and keep watching. More information is often on its way. It's not that you misunderstood the sign, but that the meaning has not yet fully unfolded.

Spiritual communication often arrives in layers. The first sign might awaken curiosity. The next confirms a direction. And another might clarify the exact timing. Acting on the first impulse without allowing space for the rest of the message to come through can lead to frustration. Patience allows you to receive the full transmission rather than jumping to conclusions based on the first line of a message.

If you find yourself unclear, it is always wise to ask. Ask your own inner guidance for clarity. Ask life to confirm or clarify the next move. And then pay attention—not only to what appears, but how it feels when it appears. Your job is not to chase signs until they become clear. Your job is to stay in a posture of receptivity, knowing that clarity often arrives when you are ready to hold it.

Waiting, when approached with presence, is not a passive state. It is an active form of listening. It requires trust that something is in motion even if you can't see it. Often, the impulse to act comes not from clarity, but from discomfort with uncertainty. We try to fill the space with movement, hoping that doing something will resolve the tension. But signs sometimes arrive precisely to slow you down, to bring your awareness back to yourself before you rush into the next thing. This kind of pause is sacred. It allows life to unfold without force.

It's important to learn the difference between waiting with intention and avoiding action. Avoidance usually carries an undercurrent of fear, doubt, or indecision. It feels heavy or dull. You might feel stuck in loops of overthinking, hoping to delay a choice indefinitely. Waiting, on the other hand, feels quieter. It's more like being rooted, still and attentive, ready to move when the signal is clear. Your intuition stays active in this state, not shut down. You're not postponing out of fear. You're allowing the pieces to come together naturally.

One way to anchor yourself during these periods is to stay open without pressing for resolution. Keep noticing. Keep asking. Keep listening. And stay in movement internally, even if there's no external decision to make. You may be integrating something, or being prepared for something that is not yet in reach. In these moments, the best you can do is hold your center, stay close to yourself, and allow life to reveal the next step without trying to force it into shape.

There may also be moments when signs appear during periods of stillness as a form of reassurance rather than instruction. You may see repeated affirmations, comforting images, or symbols that mirror your inner state. These are reminders that you're not off track just because things are quiet. The absence of action is not the absence of movement. Inner growth, recalibration, and realignment often happen when nothing visible seems to be occurring.

When the time to act does come, it often arrives with a kind of clarity that doesn't need to be analyzed. It may not be dramatic or loud, but it feels solid. You might suddenly know what to do, or you might find the opportunity presenting itself without resistance. When your body, intuition, and circumstances all align, there's often a smoothness to the action. It doesn't feel like effort. It feels like stepping into something already unfolding.

But there are also times when action is required even in the absence of complete certainty. Sometimes the sign is the nudge to move, and clarity follows movement. In those cases, the sign acts as a spark. You may still feel fear or hesitation, but underneath it is a pulse of readiness. This is where courage meets faith. Not every action comes wrapped in total confidence. But there is a difference between fear that warns and fear that protects. When fear arises but is not rooted in misalignment, it may be a sign that growth is near.

The deeper you go into your own spiritual communication, the more refined this discernment becomes. You start recognizing how your signals feel in the body, how your intuition speaks when it's time, and how your emotions shift between readiness and resistance. No external rule can substitute for the inner clarity that emerges when you learn to trust this process.

The dance between acting and waiting is part of the larger rhythm of your life. You are not meant to live in constant momentum, nor are you meant to remain indefinitely still. The wisdom lies in honoring each phase as it comes. When the sign is clear, act with heart. When it is incomplete, wait with trust. Both are sacred. Both are necessary.

Navigating Conflicting Signals

Conflicting signals are one of the most confusing aspects of spiritual communication. You may feel deeply drawn in one direction, only to receive what seems like a warning or contradiction. One sign might feel like encouragement, while another feels like a red light. This can create emotional tension, inner doubt, and a sense of paralysis. The truth is, receiving mixed messages is not necessarily a sign that your intuition is broken. It often means your inner system is processing multiple layers at once, and you are being invited to pause, listen deeper, and sort through the noise with care.

The first thing to understand is that not all signs carry the same weight. Just because something appears first or most often doesn't make it the most reliable. Some signs may come from fear-based expectations, from unhealed wounds, or from projections of the mind. Others may come from your soul's deeper knowing. Discerning the source of a signal is essential, and that discernment comes from practice, not from perfection.

One helpful step is to sit with each conflicting message on its own, without trying to reconcile them immediately. Instead of jumping to action or shutting one of them down, give each signal space to be felt fully. Ask yourself: What does this sign bring up in me? Does it feel expansive or constricting? Calm or chaotic? Is there a part of me that wants to believe this because it aligns with my fear, or does it awaken something deeper and quieter in me?

You might also notice that different parts of you are being activated by different signals. One part may crave safety, stability, or approval. Another may be longing for growth, truth, or freedom. When these inner voices aren't aligned, your external signs often mirror the internal split. The confusion is not a punishment. It's a mirror. Something within you is asking to be integrated before you move forward with clarity.

Sometimes what seems like a conflict is actually a sequence. You might receive a sign to move forward, followed by a warning. That doesn't always mean the first sign was wrong. It may mean you need to prepare before taking that step. Or that you are meant to go in that direction, but not yet. The apparent contradiction may be resolved by shifting your timing, your method, or your inner readiness.

In other moments, the conflict comes from comparing external signs with internal resistance. You may see synchronicities pointing in a certain direction, but feel uneasy or heavy about following them. This dissonance deserves attention. It could be that the path is right, but your nervous system is overwhelmed. It could also be that the signs you're seeing are real, but not meant for you to act on yet. Timing, again, plays a critical role. The universe does not always speak in a straight line. It speaks in waves, rhythms, and echoes that require interpretation.

The key is not to force resolution too quickly. You are not failing if things feel unclear. You are learning how to stay with the discomfort of not-knowing, while still remaining curious and available. When signals conflict, it's not a call to shut down. It's an invitation to listen more closely, to become more honest with yourself, and to wait for your clarity to become undeniable.

The ability to navigate conflicting signals is not about forcing clarity but cultivating a deeper intimacy with your own inner language. One of the most grounding tools in these moments is radical honesty. Ask yourself not only what the signs are saying but also what you truly want them to say. Are you looking for confirmation of a decision you've already made? Are you resisting one path because it feels risky, even if it's right? Self-inquiry can strip away the layers of projection and reveal the voice beneath the noise.

Another helpful approach is to create stillness. When you're flooded with mixed messages, the nervous system often reacts by trying to resolve things too fast. But rushing leads to distortion. Instead, let yourself pause. Disconnect from external input for a moment. Go inward. Breathe deeply, drop into your body, and notice what sensations arise when you place your awareness on each possible direction. Often, your body knows what your mind is afraid to admit. Tension, constriction, or a sense of collapse can signal that something is out of alignment. Warmth, relaxation, or grounded energy can indicate inner truth.

Patterns can also clarify confusion. If you've seen a particular signal multiple times in different settings over a sustained period, and it consistently evokes a certain emotional response, that's worth noting. But one-time flashes or emotionally charged "signs" that provoke panic are less likely to be grounded in wisdom. Emotional reactivity is not the same as intuitive knowing. Learning to tell the difference between these states is essential.

In rare cases, conflicting signals might be testing your level of commitment. The universe sometimes offers mixed messages to help you clarify what you truly desire. If both options have their appeal, but one leaves you uncertain and the other lights up your core, even while challenging you, the real sign may be the one you're most afraid to follow. Fear often wraps itself around the most important truths. Instead of looking for the signal that feels safest, look for the one that feels most alive.

Journaling can be a powerful tool to unravel confusion. Write down each signal you received, when and how it appeared, what emotion it stirred, and what inner part it seemed to speak to. Then, reflect. Is there a thread connecting them? Do they all point to the same deeper question? What would happen if you didn't try to resolve the conflict right away but instead held space for both messages to sit side by side? Sometimes the answer is not either-or. Sometimes both are true in different ways, and the real invitation is to find a third path that honors both.

Ultimately, the ability to move through conflicting signals depends on your willingness to trust the process. That means trusting that confusion itself is part of the path, not a detour. It means accepting that clarity sometimes comes only after surrender, not before. And it means building a relationship with uncertainty that is not adversarial but reverent. When you treat confusion as sacred, you stop needing to rush it away. You begin to listen more deeply, soften more fully, and eventually, the truth becomes clear not through force, but through resonance.

Learning to live with this kind of discernment will strengthen your connection with higher guidance. It sharpens your intuition, deepens your patience, and teaches you that spiritual communication is not always clean and linear. It is often layered, nuanced, and shaped by the level of inner coherence you are cultivating. When that coherence grows, the mixed signals settle, and what once felt like contradiction begins to organize into clarity. And from that clarity, action becomes not just possible, but empowered.

Trusting Yourself in the Face of Doubt

Doubt has a way of sneaking in when you need clarity most. Just when you're beginning to trust a sign, a choice, or a subtle inner pull, the voice of uncertainty can rise like a tide, whispering questions that sound logical but feel heavy. This is part of the human experience, especially when you're walking a path led by intuition rather than external validation. Trusting yourself is not about silencing doubt forever, but about learning how to move through it without collapsing your center.

To begin cultivating that trust, it helps to understand where doubt comes from. Often, it's not a true warning sign from your higher self but a conditioned reflex. Doubt is learned. It's reinforced by years of being told to defer to experts, to follow rules, to second-guess instinct in favor of logic. Over time, this creates a disconnect. You begin to doubt not because you are wrong, but because you have been taught that certainty must be justified with proof.

But the inner knowing that guides your path does not always come with external evidence. It often speaks quietly, through felt sensations, sudden clarity, or subtle alignment that can't be easily explained. When doubt arises in those moments, it's rarely because your intuition has failed. More often, it's because your old programming has been activated. Recognizing this is the first step in reclaiming self-trust.

You don't need to wait for the absence of fear or confusion before trusting yourself. Real trust includes those feelings. It doesn't pretend they're not there. Instead, it gives them space without handing over the wheel. You can hold doubt in one hand and your truth in the other. You can feel uncertainty in your body and still know that something is right for you, even if others don't understand or approve.

The key is to practice listening beyond the mental noise. When doubt shows up, don't try to silence it immediately. Be curious. Ask yourself where it comes from. Is it rooted in past disappointment? A fear of failure? A desire for perfection? Naming the source of your doubt can separate it from your current moment. It creates breathing room between the fear and your truth.

You can also return to your body as an anchor. Trust is often felt somatically before it's known mentally. A grounded sense of ease, an open breath, a peaceful stillness—these are signs that your body is aligned with the path, even when your mind is spiraling with questions. When the body says yes, it's usually wise to pay attention, especially if the doubt you feel is tangled in imagined futures or external opinions.

Learning to trust yourself also involves revisiting your past. There have been moments when you knew, and that knowing turned out to be right. Even if you doubted it at the time, the truth eventually revealed itself. Make space to recall those moments. Write them down. Feel them again. Let them remind you that your inner compass has worked before, and it's still working now.

This doesn't mean you'll never make a mistake. But trusting yourself is not about guaranteeing perfect outcomes. It's about choosing alignment, even when the path is uncertain. It's about honoring what feels whole, honest, and true in you, regardless of the reaction it might provoke. And when you trust that kind of truth, the need to control every step softens. You become willing to walk with openness instead of fear.

When you practice this level of presence, you start to notice how often doubt is a reaction rather than a revelation. It usually follows a moment of clarity, not precedes it. You feel something true in your body, a quiet yes, and then the old patterns flood in. This sequence is important to recognize. It shows that doubt is not the origin of your knowing but a challenge to it. And like any challenge, it becomes easier to face when you're not trying to defeat it, but simply walk beside it.

What often helps is to give yourself permission not to have full certainty before you move. Clarity doesn't always come all at once. Sometimes, you gain confidence step by step, after taking the first action. Waiting for doubt to completely disappear before you act can keep you stuck in a loop. But if you allow movement, even in small ways, you create space for trust to grow naturally, through experience.

There's also wisdom in understanding that your intuition may not always give you linear instructions. It might nudge you toward something that doesn't immediately make sense, but later proves essential. This is why trusting yourself means being available to mystery. Not everything will be clear in advance. Sometimes, all you have is a thread of resonance, a deep pull toward a direction that your mind can't yet explain. That's enough. That's valid.

You don't have to share your inner guidance with everyone. Trusting yourself doesn't require convincing others. In fact, trying to seek approval for what your soul already knows can erode your confidence. Protect your knowing while it's still tender. Let it deepen in private. Let it become so familiar and integrated that you no longer need outside permission to follow it.

What you'll notice over time is that trust creates a feedback loop. Each time you listen to yourself and honor that inner nudge, even in small decisions, the signal gets stronger. You begin to recognize your own energetic signature of truth. It has a texture. A tone. A presence. The more you engage with it, the more quickly you'll know when something is aligned and when it's not. Doubt becomes quieter. Not absent, but no longer dominant.

On the days when doubt feels overwhelming, remember that self-trust doesn't mean having all the answers. It means being willing to stay with yourself no matter what arises. You don't have to figure it all out right away. You just have to stay connected. Breathe. Listen. Stay open. That's the practice. And over time, it becomes a kind of inner sanctuary. A place you return to again and again, even when everything else is uncertain.

Eventually, trusting yourself becomes less about evaluating whether your feelings are valid and more about honoring that they are present. You stop questioning if your sensitivity is too much, or your inner sense too unreliable. You understand that this is your guidance system, and it's been speaking to you all along. What once felt like confusion becomes part of your deeper clarity.

The more you lean in, the more you realize that self-trust is not just a tool for making decisions. It's a relationship. One that requires care, patience, and presence. One that will evolve as you grow. But the foundation remains the same: you are the authority on your inner world. No one else can interpret your signs, your path, or your truth better than you.

And when you embrace that, even with the doubt sitting beside you, you become unshakeable in a quiet way. Not because you're always right, but because you're always listening. Because you are willing to stay close to what feels honest, even when it's uncomfortable. That's what makes the difference. That's what makes it real.

Part IV — Living in Alignment with Guidance

There comes a point in your journey with signs, intuition, and subtle messages when seeking clarity is no longer just a practice. It becomes a way of life. You begin to move differently. You pause before reacting. You notice the energy behind people's words, the timing of events, the echo of meaning in the ordinary. Life no longer feels random or separate from your inner world. It becomes a conversation. A mirror. A flow.

This part of the path is about integration. It's not about collecting more signs or decoding every coincidence. It's about embodying the guidance you've already received. About living from the quiet inner alignment you've been cultivating. When you reach this place, spiritual awareness is no longer something you turn on during meditation or reflection. It begins to show up in how you speak, decide, rest, create, and relate. It weaves into your daily rhythm, not as something to perform, but as something to return to, again and again.

Living in alignment does not mean becoming perfect. It doesn't mean you'll never doubt, resist, or forget. It means you begin to recognize when you're out of sync, and you know how to come back. You start to trust that your inner compass works, not because it gives you all the answers, but because it keeps you connected to the truth of your own experience. You rely less on outside validation and more on your felt sense of what resonates.

In this final part of the book, we'll explore what it looks like to walk with guidance at your side. Not as a special skill or rare moment, but as a grounded orientation to life. You'll learn how to stay tuned to your inner clarity when external pressures pull you in different directions. You'll discover how to make decisions from a place of truth, even when others don't understand. And you'll begin to build a life that reflects what you know deep down: that your path is sacred, your intuition is trustworthy, and your presence has meaning.

The work ahead is subtle, but powerful. It's not about doing more. It's about being more attuned, more honest, more available to what already wants to move through you. This is not the end of your journey with signs. It's the beginning of a new way of living—one in which you don't just read the messages, but embody their wisdom.

You've already seen the signs. Now it's time to live as if they mattered.

Chapter 10: Building a Daily Signs Practice

Morning and Evening Routines to Stay Tuned In

How you begin and end your day matters more than most people realize. These are the two most energetically open windows you experience in a twenty-four-hour cycle. Your body is in transition. Your subconscious is active. Your emotional state is more impressionable. It is during these times that you have a unique opportunity to align yourself intentionally with the guidance that already surrounds you. When your days are bookended with awareness, clarity naturally becomes a part of your rhythm.

A morning routine doesn't have to be long or complicated to be effective. What it must be is conscious. Most people start their day by reaching for their phone, checking messages, or diving into tasks before they've had a chance to remember who they are. This sets the tone for a reactive day. If your first inputs are noise, demands, or disconnection, it becomes much harder to receive the subtler cues of intuition throughout the day. It's like trying to hear a whisper in the middle of a crowded room.

Instead, imagine starting your morning by giving yourself just ten minutes of quiet presence. No expectations, no pressure to perform. Just time to listen inwardly. Sit in stillness. Pay attention to how your body feels. Scan gently for emotional tones that are already present. Before doing anything, give yourself permission to check in with the part of you that holds truth without noise.

One powerful way to amplify this connection is by engaging with a simple morning anchoring question. For example: "What truth do I need to carry today?" or "What is the energy I choose to walk in?" Let the answers arise softly. They may come as words, images, sensations, or even silence. Sometimes, clarity isn't in the content but in the pause itself. Movement can also be part of tuning in. You don't need a full workout. Even a few mindful stretches, a short walk in the morning air, or placing your bare feet on the floor with intention can help you feel embodied.

When your body is awake, your awareness sharpens. You start to notice the subtleties around you: how light moves in your room, how your breath shifts, how you instinctively feel about the day ahead.

Once this connection is made, you can carry it forward as a subtle thread that stays with you. You may still get distracted, stressed, or thrown off, but returning becomes easier when the day begins with clarity. You start from alignment rather than scrambling to find it.

Evening routines serve a different but equally vital purpose. If the morning is for setting your direction, the evening is for releasing what is not yours and integrating what the day has offered. Most people carry the weight of their day into their sleep. Their minds stay restless. Their nervous systems remain activated. This creates a cycle where sleep becomes recovery from chaos rather than a space for restoration and insight.

You don't need elaborate rituals. What you need is space to close the loop. A few moments to scan through the day and notice where your energy went, where your attention lingered, and whether you honored the guidance you felt. This is not about judgment or perfection. It's about building a relationship with your inner world that is honest, curious, and responsive.

You might sit with a journal and write down any moments that stood out. Maybe something unusual happened, a symbol appeared, or you felt a deep pull toward a person or idea. By capturing these fragments, you begin to build a language with the unseen parts of your life. You create continuity between days, which is how signs often unfold.

Reflection before sleep is most powerful when approached with softness rather than scrutiny. Instead of dissecting what you should have done differently, shift toward presence. Ask yourself simple questions that allow you to reconnect. Was there a moment today when you ignored a nudge? Did something feel off, and you moved past it too quickly? Was there a time when you felt deeply aligned, even if just for a moment? These inquiries help the inner dialogue stay alive and grow more honest over time.

It also helps to consciously release anything that isn't yours. Without realizing it, you may be carrying emotions or energies from people, situations, or environments that don't belong to you. The nervous system can hold onto tension that wasn't generated by your own thoughts. Taking even one minute to breathe deeply and declare your intent to let go of what doesn't serve can shift your internal state. Letting go is a quiet art, but over time, it becomes an instinct that protects your clarity.

Another tool that reinforces evening alignment is visualization. Picture the energy of your day gathering into a thread. Watch what you want to carry into tomorrow. See yourself placing what matters into your heart, and letting the rest dissolve. This isn't fantasy or escapism. It's energetic hygiene. When you sleep with intention, your subconscious processes more efficiently. Your dreams speak more clearly. Your waking hours feel less fragmented.

Some people find it helpful to create a symbolic signal that marks the end of the day. It could be lighting a candle, turning off devices with a specific affirmation, or simply placing a hand on the heart with a silent commitment to peace. What matters is the consistency. Your body and energy field begin to associate these small actions with safety, closure, and reset. Over time, this calms anxiety and sharpens intuition.

None of these practices require perfection. Some days you may forget. Some nights you may fall asleep mid-thought. What matters is returning. This is not about control. It's about trust. You are learning to live in harmony with subtle currents that guide you, and this requires kindness toward yourself. Rigidity creates more noise. Grace creates space for truth.

There may also be mornings when you wake with heaviness, or evenings when clarity feels out of reach. In those moments, it's enough to simply be with what is. You are not meant to extract a message from every breath. Some seasons are quieter than others. Stillness can be a sign too. The absence of clarity is not failure. Sometimes it is a pause that prepares you for deeper alignment.

The more you engage with your mornings and evenings as sacred gateways, the more you begin to see your life as a sequence of invitations. Guidance is not just in symbols and synchronicities, but also in the rhythm of your own breath, the quality of your rest, the tone of your inner voice. These are not separate from the signs you seek. They are part of the same system. Your system.

Eventually, you stop looking for signs out there and start recognizing them within. You become less concerned with asking for proof and more open to noticing what is already being offered. And with that, your routines shift from obligation to devotion. They become a form of communion with your own truth.

This is what it means to stay tuned in. Not to be perfect. Not to be always certain. But to be willing, open, and steady. Morning after morning. Night after night. Attuning to the quiet intelligence that never really leaves you. It only waits for you to return.

How to Ask for Clear Guidance

Asking for guidance is not about begging the universe for answers. It's about stepping into conscious relationship with the unseen. It begins not with pleading, but with presence. If your energy is frantic, scattered, or rooted in fear, the signals you receive are more likely to mirror that confusion. But when you center yourself first, when you approach with sincerity and stillness, the clarity you're seeking begins to form.

The first step is internal alignment. Before asking anything, take time to drop into yourself. This doesn't need to be ceremonial or complex. Just slow down. Close your eyes. Feel your body. Breathe into the belly and soften the muscles around your chest. Let yourself arrive fully into the moment. Guidance doesn't flow well into a space that is tight, rushed, or filled with mental noise. It requires a foundation of receptivity.

Once centered, begin by naming what you truly want to understand. Often people ask vague questions and receive vague signs in return. If your question is general, like "What should I do?" or "Am I on the right path?", the answers may feel equally unspecific. Clarity in asking leads to clarity in receiving. Try narrowing it down. "Is this opportunity in alignment with my purpose?" or "Does this connection feel true to my deeper self?" Framing the question in this way helps your intuition know where to focus.

But there's more to asking than just wording. The energy behind your question matters just as much. If you're demanding proof out of fear, you may get silence. If you're trying to manipulate a certain outcome, your request is no longer honest. The universe does not respond well to coercion. It responds to alignment. Ask from a place of trust, not panic. Surrender the outcome. You are not ordering a sign as if it were a delivery. You are inviting insight from a greater intelligence.

One powerful approach is to ask for confirmation in a way that's unmistakable to you. Not so much to "test" the universe, but to enter into a deeper dialogue. You might say something like, "If I'm meant to move forward with this, show me a specific symbol that I personally associate with truth or comfort." The more personal the request, the more likely the response will feel meaningful.

124

Be mindful, though, not to treat this process as a game. Repeatedly asking the same question over and over—hoping for a different answer—only clutters your connection. Doubt is natural, but obsessive checking often reveals a lack of trust in your own capacity to hear. At some point, you must be willing to receive the answer, even if it's not the one your ego wants.

Sometimes, the clearest answers arise not from asking outwardly, but from listening inwardly. After asking your question, sit in stillness for a few minutes. Pay attention to what surfaces in your body. Is there tightness? Expansion? Resistance? Ease? Your body is often the first to speak. Even before a sign appears in the world, your system is already registering the deeper truth.

Dreams may also carry responses. After your request, consider setting the intention to receive guidance while sleeping. You don't need to force a message to arrive overnight, but simply create a soft opening: "If there's something I need to know, I'm open to seeing it clearly in a dream." Then release the expectation. Trust that clarity may come when you're not trying so hard to find it.

Sometimes no sign will appear at all. This can feel frustrating or disheartening, but silence is not the same as absence. In fact, a lack of immediate response is often guidance in itself. It may mean the decision is truly yours to make, that both paths hold value, or that the timing isn't right yet. Waiting is not a punishment. It can be an invitation to deepen your inner trust, to let the need for external confirmation dissolve, and to stand fully in your own authority.

Other times, the sign comes but is missed because it doesn't look how you expected. You might be waiting for a feather to fall in your path when instead a sentence overheard in a conversation strikes your heart with precision. Or you might be hoping for a dream but instead feel an unexpected peace the moment you let go of overthinking. Remaining open to the unexpected is key. The more attached you are to how the guidance *should* look, the harder it will be to recognize it when it actually arrives.

After receiving something that feels like a sign, the next step is not to panic or overanalyze. It's to notice how it lands within you. Is there a sense of resonance, of internal yes, of a sudden clarity or softening? Or do you feel even more confused, constricted, or unsettled? Your emotional and somatic response will often reveal more than the content of the sign itself. Clarity doesn't always feel comfortable, but it will usually feel *true*.

You may also find that guidance comes in layers. A single sign might not carry the full answer, but rather act as a nudge, pointing you in a direction that becomes clearer as you move. You take one step, and then the next cue reveals itself. Asking for guidance, then, is rarely a one-time event. It's a living conversation that unfolds over time. Your part is to keep showing up with honesty, curiosity, and patience.

It's also worth noting that sometimes, the clearest form of guidance is not symbolic at all. It's an inner knowing that arises before a question is even asked. In those moments, asking for external signs might feel redundant. This is not arrogance, but intimacy. When your alignment with yourself is deep, the need for confirmation fades. You begin to move from a quieter confidence, the kind that doesn't ask to be proven right, because it already feels anchored.

Still, asking can be a beautiful practice when used with integrity. It keeps you humble, engaged, and relational with the world around you. It reminds you that you are not alone, and that life itself wants to participate in your unfolding. But don't mistake the process for a transaction. This is not about performance. It's about learning to speak and listen across visible and invisible layers of reality.

Trust will grow through experience. You'll ask, you'll receive, and over time, patterns will form. You'll notice how your guidance tends to arrive, what states of mind allow for clearer answers, and what inner habits tend to block your ability to hear. Journaling can support this, not as a ritual of control, but as a way to reflect and witness the subtle language that emerges between you and the world.

Asking for clear guidance is not about seeking guarantees. It's about entering into a dialogue with the deeper intelligence that runs beneath your thoughts. When you treat that dialogue with reverence and clarity, when you bring your whole self to it without demand, something in the unseen begins to respond. Not always instantly. Not always with the answer you expect. But always with the invitation to trust more deeply. And that, often, is the guidance that matters most.

Staying Open Without Becoming Obsessive

There is a fine line between receptivity and obsession, and learning how to walk that line is one of the most important aspects of working with spiritual signs. Openness is the quality of being available to receive guidance, to notice synchronicities, to live in dialogue with the world around you. Obsession, on the other hand, emerges when the search for meaning becomes rigid, compulsive, or fear-driven. One is anchored in trust. The other in control.

Staying open begins with a calm, steady presence. It means allowing signs to appear without chasing them. When your nervous system is regulated, you're more likely to notice subtle patterns and nudges. But when your body is in a constant state of hypervigilance, scanning every moment for clues or omens, the signal gets drowned out by noise. The clarity you're seeking becomes harder to access, not because guidance isn't present, but because your energy is clouded by anxiety.

Openness is not passive, but it's also not forceful. It's receptive awareness paired with grounded discernment. It's asking for a sign and then releasing the outcome, rather than checking the clock every five minutes, replaying every conversation, or scrolling endlessly through symbolic meanings online. This kind of mental looping doesn't bring more clarity. It often leads to confusion, doubt, and spiritual fatigue.

There's also a subtle form of obsession that comes disguised as devotion. You might think you're being committed to your path, showing spiritual diligence by cataloging every event, analyzing every dream, or meticulously journaling every possible message. But beneath that intensity, there can sometimes be a fear of missing something important. A belief that if you don't pay attention constantly, you'll fall out of alignment or make the wrong choice. This fear tightens the body and narrows your intuitive channel.

True openness is spacious. It allows for not knowing. It makes room for mystery. It doesn't need to solve everything immediately. In fact, many of the most meaningful signs arrive in moments of surrender, when you're not watching the skies for symbols but simply living your life with presence. You're on a walk, making breakfast, having a quiet conversation, and then something clicks. A sentence lands. A number repeats. A knowing arrives. And because you're not gripping, you're able to recognize it for what it is.

To stay open without becoming obsessive, you have to learn how to hold your curiosity with soft hands. You can ask questions, but don't demand answers. You can listen for guidance, but don't micromanage the conversation. You can set intentions, but let them breathe. This inner stance cultivates a deep confidence in the relationship you have with the unseen. You stop treating life as a puzzle to solve, and instead allow meaning to emerge in its own rhythm.

One of the most effective ways to do this is by focusing on your lived experience rather than constantly trying to interpret it. Ground yourself in the now. Feel your breath. Stay connected to your senses. If a symbol appears, take note, but don't spin into analysis immediately. Let it sit. Let it unfold. If it's real guidance, it will stay with you. It will return. It will grow louder or repeat until you feel it in your bones. You won't need to overthink it. Your body will recognize it.

The mind often craves certainty, and that craving can disguise itself as a spiritual pursuit. You might feel the need to "get it right," to interpret everything perfectly, to avoid missteps by decoding the signs with absolute accuracy. But this desire is often rooted in fear, not faith. It's a way of trying to control the uncontrollable. When you're operating from this place, even the most innocent signs become burdens. Instead of offering support or insight, they become one more thing to figure out, one more pressure to interpret flawlessly.

To soften that edge, remind yourself that your relationship with signs is not a test. There's no cosmic scoreboard keeping track of whether you understood the meaning of a number or acted quickly enough on an intuitive nudge. Guidance doesn't disappear because you missed a cue. In fact, when something matters, it often circles back in another form. The universe is not impatient. It's not punitive. It's patient and persistent, always working with your readiness.

You're allowed to miss something. You're allowed to not be sure. You're allowed to say, "I'm not clear yet," and wait. That humility opens doors that forcefulness cannot. It also helps you develop deeper trust in yourself. When you stop obsessing over the external sign and begin paying attention to how it moves within you, you become less dependent on external confirmations and more anchored in inner knowing.

It's also important to recognize when you're using signs to avoid making a decision. If you find yourself asking for repeated signs about the same thing, hoping for a different answer, it might be a signal that you already know what you need to do, but you're afraid to act. In that case, the pursuit of guidance becomes a stall tactic. It's not wrong to want reassurance. But growth often asks us to act with incomplete information, to move forward even when the path isn't lit from end to end.

Learning to stay open without falling into obsession means honoring your intuition as much as the sign itself. If a symbol feels significant, but the timing isn't right, you don't need to act impulsively. If no signs appear for a while, you're not disconnected. Sometimes, silence is guidance. Sometimes, the clearest answer is found in the quiet space between signs, where you are asked to trust the path you're already on.

Cultivating this balanced approach takes practice. It means being willing to be surprised. It means letting go of timelines. It means resisting the urge to interpret everything immediately. It means staying grounded in your daily life, even as you remain open to the extraordinary. When you do this, your spiritual sensitivity doesn't diminish. It sharpens. Not through effort, but through attunement. You become the kind of person who notices the breeze shift, who hears the deeper meaning behind a passing phrase, who knows how to pause and wait for the message to ripen.

You don't need to search constantly. You need to live attentively. Let your life be the signal. Let your peace be the sign. Let your presence be the prayer that keeps you open without gripping, listening without leaning, receiving without chasing. That's the posture of true alignment. That's how you stay open and stay free.

Chapter 11: When the Signs Go Quiet

What Silence Means in the Spiritual Dialogue

There will come moments on your path when everything goes quiet. No numbers. No dreams. No perfectly timed lyrics or overheard phrases. No intuitive nudges that feel charged or clear. Just stillness. It can feel unsettling, even disorienting, especially after a period where signs seemed to flow easily and consistently. You may begin to wonder if you've done something wrong or drifted off course. You might even question whether you're still being guided at all.

But silence is not absence. Silence is presence in another form. It is part of the language of the divine. Not all communication arrives in the form of answers. Sometimes, the silence *is* the message.

In a world filled with noise, our instinct is to fill the quiet, to seek explanations, to ask again. We've been conditioned to equate clarity with constant input. But spiritual communication operates on a different rhythm. It unfolds not by speed, but by depth. In many cases, silence is a sacred invitation to listen differently, to turn inward rather than outward, and to recalibrate your understanding of guidance itself.

Silence may be asking you to trust what you already know. When you've received a sign and then everything seems to go still, it's often not because guidance has stopped, but because it's now time to integrate what you've been shown. There's a difference between receiving a message and living it. The silence gives you space to take aligned action without needing constant reinforcement. It's a way of building spiritual maturity, the kind that doesn't rely on a steady stream of validation but instead roots itself in quiet faith.

There's also a protective quality to silence. If you're in a place where your energy is scattered, your emotions are running high, or your mind is spinning with anxiety, silence may act as a buffer. Not because you're being punished, but because clear interpretation can't happen in a storm. Just as a radio signal needs clarity to be received without distortion, so too does spiritual guidance require a certain stillness within you. Silence can be a kind of grace, giving you room to return to yourself before the next message arrives.

Sometimes, silence is simply an answer in itself. It may be saying, "There's nothing more to add right now." Or, "This is not your question to ask." Or even, "You already hold the answer." But because it lacks dramatic flair, silence is often mistaken for abandonment. It's not. It's a form of deep listening—on both sides.

If you find yourself in a silent season, resist the urge to force meaning. Instead, observe what's happening in your life without judgment. Pay attention to your emotions, your dreams, the quality of your inner voice. Even when nothing seems to be happening on the surface, your inner world is still in motion. Growth often happens in the quiet. Seeds germinate in darkness, and clarity takes shape in stillness long before it becomes visible.

This kind of silence invites you to remember that spiritual dialogue is not transactional. It's relational. And relationships include pauses. They include moments when nothing needs to be said, because the connection itself is enough. Trust can deepen not through more information, but through a willingness to remain present when nothing is being said at all.

It's also important to remember that silence can point you toward self-reliance. In the early stages of a spiritual journey, signs often appear frequently, almost as if you're being taught a new language. But as you develop fluency, there comes a time when you're expected to speak it for yourself. The silence, then, isn't neglect. It's trust. It's the universe saying, "You're ready to apply what you've learned without hand-holding." You are not being left behind. You are being empowered to step forward.

This kind of empowerment can feel lonely. Without the usual cues, you may question your path. But inner clarity doesn't always announce itself. It settles in like a presence that doesn't need to prove anything. That's the kind of quiet you begin to feel when you stop trying to chase a message and instead begin living in alignment with your knowing. Often, the loudest confirmation is a calm certainty that doesn't beg for signs anymore. It just moves.

Silence may also be the space where your deeper intuition begins to take root. When you're not looking for signs everywhere, your inner compass becomes sharper. You start to recognize that some answers aren't given in advance because they require your full presence to be discovered moment by moment. Life stops being a puzzle to decode and becomes a relationship to participate in. You begin to walk with life instead of looking ahead for instructions.

In some instances, silence can be the result of asking from a place of fear or control. When your desire for guidance is driven by anxiety, it can cloud the spiritual channel. Not because the divine doesn't respond, but because panic short-circuits reception. The guidance is still present, but it's waiting for you to shift your posture from desperation to openness. From needing to know everything right now to being willing to wait and trust. The message might not be withheld. It might just be waiting for you to become still enough to hear it.

When silence stretches, it can also be an invitation to reset your focus. Maybe your attention has become fixed on something you want but is no longer aligned. Maybe you've drifted toward grasping rather than receiving. The absence of signs can feel like a void, but sometimes that void is where realignment happens. In the quiet, you can start asking deeper questions. Not just "What should I do?" but "What am I becoming?" Not just "Where is my sign?" but "Where is my center?"

If silence is teaching you anything, it's patience. The kind of patience that isn't passive or resigned, but open, alert, and tender. You begin to feel into timing rather than push against it. You realize that spiritual connection isn't a series of events. It's a way of being. And being doesn't always talk.

So when everything goes quiet, don't panic. Don't retreat. Sit with it. Breathe into it. Keep living your life with as much integrity, clarity, and presence as you can. If something needs to be known, it will reveal itself. If a shift is needed, it will come. If a door is to open, you won't miss it. The silence is not your enemy. It is the deep breath before the next unfolding. Trust it. Let it teach you to listen not just for what is said, but for what is felt. Not just for signs in the world, but for peace within your own soul.

Seasons of Waiting, Growth, or Hidden Alignment

There are times in life when everything seems to pause. No breakthroughs, no clear direction, no dramatic inner nudges. You might feel like you're doing everything right—staying open, tuning in, following your intuition—and yet, the external results are minimal, the signs feel faint or nonexistent, and you begin to question if you've somehow gone off track. But not all pauses are a sign of misalignment. Some are sacred intervals of preparation, healing, or quiet transformation. These are what we call seasons of waiting, growth, or hidden alignment.

In modern life, we are conditioned to expect immediate outcomes. If we plant something, we want it to bloom tomorrow. If we ask for a sign, we want it now. But the natural world operates differently. A tree does not sprout overnight. Its roots dig deep before its branches rise. In spiritual terms, the same principle applies. Some shifts require stillness. Some blessings arrive only when the ground of your being is ready to hold them.

A season of waiting is not wasted time. It is often where the most profound shifts happen below the surface. You might be integrating experiences, shedding outdated beliefs, or being refined in ways your conscious mind cannot fully grasp yet. On the outside, nothing appears to be changing. On the inside, you are becoming someone new. The quiet is not empty. It is full of unseen activity. This is when faith matures—not in the form of blind optimism, but through the practice of inner trust.

In these periods, impatience can be the biggest saboteur. The temptation is to force something to happen. To jump ahead just to feel in motion again. But spiritual alignment is not maintained through constant effort. It is maintained through attunement. When you are in tune with the rhythm of your own life, you stop comparing your path to others. You recognize that your timeline is not broken just because it is not fast.

Growth often happens in disguise. You may not feel strong, but you are strengthening. You may not feel wise, but you are gaining wisdom. A setback may be the very thing that builds resilience. A delay might be protecting you from something you're not yet ready to carry. Growth does not always feel like growth. Sometimes it feels like grief, confusion, or stagnation. But if you stay present, if you stay willing, if you keep tending to your inner world even without reward, something starts to shift.

Hidden alignment is one of the most underestimated forces in the spiritual journey. Just because you can't see how the pieces are fitting together doesn't mean they aren't. Sometimes, life rearranges itself in the background. People shift. Opportunities form. Conditions align quietly, and then, suddenly, you find yourself in the right place at the right time without having pushed your way there. That is not coincidence. That is the result of a deeper intelligence operating on your behalf while you were faithful to your part.

This kind of alignment requires humility. You are not in control of the entire picture. You are in relationship with it. Your role is not to dictate the timing of outcomes, but to participate in the unfolding of your own becoming. There is a rhythm to your life, and sometimes it slows down to teach you how to listen. Sometimes it stops so you can catch up to yourself. These pauses are not detours. They are initiations.

You may be tempted to fill the silence with noise or to busy yourself with plans just to avoid the discomfort of stillness. But these seasons ask for a different kind of courage. They ask you to sit in the unknown and trust that something meaningful is unfolding beyond your current comprehension. This kind of waiting is not passive. It is engaged presence. It is the quiet work of staying open, even when nothing is confirming your path. It is choosing not to shut down just because the evidence hasn't arrived yet.

You might feel as if your prayers or intentions have been lost in a void. But stillness is not absence. In many sacred traditions, silence is where the divine voice speaks most clearly. When there are no distractions, the soul can rise to the surface. You may start to notice subtle shifts, small signs, brief moments of clarity. These are not random. They are threads pulling you forward, slowly but surely, toward the next step of your path. Rather than asking, "Why isn't anything happening?" it can be more powerful to ask, "What is this moment asking of me?" This simple reframe moves you out of resistance and into receptivity. You stop seeing waiting as punishment and begin to understand it as sacred preparation. This shift in perception is often the key to receiving the deeper meaning of the moment. It's not about bypassing your frustration, but about letting your awareness expand beyond it.

Often, you are not being withheld from your desire. You are being made into someone who can hold it. And that becoming takes time. Just like a seed cannot rush its sprouting, your growth requires a period of invisible momentum. It may feel like nothing is happening, but in the unseen layers of your being, everything is shifting. Patience in these moments is not weakness. It is spiritual stamina.

What helps is staying in relationship with your inner world. Let yourself feel what you feel without judgment. Let yourself question without rushing to an answer. Let yourself rest when clarity doesn't come. You are not failing because you don't have the next step. You are learning to trust that even silence has its role. You are learning to live not only from desire and direction, but from presence and patience.

During these seasons, your inner practices become anchors. Journaling, prayer, movement, time in nature—these are not just routines. They are ways to stay aligned with your inner knowing, even when the outer path is not fully revealed. They help you remember who you are beyond the circumstances. They help you stay grounded in truth, so that when the time for action does come, you are ready to meet it without hesitation or confusion.

Sometimes, the most important breakthroughs come just after you've released the need to control them. When you surrender your timeline, when you stop straining for a sign, when you let go of what you thought had to happen and how, you open space for life to surprise you. In that surrender, alignment often returns like breath after holding. Clear direction reappears. Pieces fall into place. And you realize the waiting was not a pause in your path. It was part of it.

There is grace in trusting that life is not only working for you when things are moving quickly. It is also working for you in the slow unfolding. In the stillness. In the spaces that feel uncertain or even empty. Alignment is not always about momentum. Sometimes it is about still roots and quiet growth. And in those moments, your greatest power is your willingness to stay present, open, and deeply faithful to your own becoming.

How to Stay Centered Without External Proof

There are moments on the spiritual path when nothing outside of you seems to validate what you feel inside. You may sense you're on the right track, deeply aligned, yet the world around you offers no confirmation. No sudden signs, no obvious rewards, no clear outcomes. This is the space where inner stability is truly forged—not through achievement, but through presence. Not through validation, but through trust.

Staying centered without external proof is one of the most advanced spiritual disciplines. It asks you to hold your truth, even when nothing outside of you echoes it back. It requires a shift from a results-based mindset to a relationship-based one. Instead of judging your alignment by what's happening, you begin to cultivate a deeper connection to how you're being.

It's easy to stay hopeful when everything is flowing. But real groundedness is born when things are still, quiet, or unclear. It is in these spaces that you are invited to anchor yourself not in outcomes, but in essence. Who are you when things don't move fast? What do you believe when your vision is not affirmed by your environment? These questions lead you to the core of spiritual maturity.

To stay centered, you must first learn to distinguish between inner knowing and outer noise. The world may be loud with opinions, expectations, and distractions. People might misunderstand your path, or even question it. The metrics that once defined success may not apply to you anymore. And that's exactly why your inner voice becomes more precious. In the absence of confirmation, you have the opportunity to make your intuition your primary compass.

This does not mean ignoring reality or bypassing logic. It means learning to value your felt sense of direction, even when the dots haven't yet connected. You may not be able to explain why a certain decision feels right, but something in your body, your heart, or your energy tells you it's aligned. Honoring that quiet clarity is not recklessness. It is integrity. It is choosing to live by your own truth, even in a world that favors proof over presence.

What makes this difficult is that we've been trained to rely on signs of success to feel safe. We look for likes, results, income, feedback, progress. When those things are missing, the mind naturally begins to doubt. But the absence of proof does not equal the absence of progress. Often, the most profound changes happen underground, invisible to the outside world. A seed doesn't show signs of life while it's building roots. You are still growing, even when nothing shows on the surface.

In these moments, your nervous system may react. You might feel anxious, restless, or tempted to quit. This is where the work is. Staying centered means building the capacity to be with discomfort without fleeing. It means noticing your need for validation, witnessing it with compassion, and choosing not to let it drive your decisions. This is not detachment. It is devotion—to your inner alignment, to your clarity, to your values.

You can support this inner centering through simple rituals that anchor you in your own energy. These don't need to be elaborate. A moment of breath before reacting. A few minutes of journaling when doubt creeps in. A gentle return to your body when your mind starts to spiral. These practices remind you that your center is not somewhere far off, but always available in the present. The more you return to it, the stronger it becomes.

When you no longer need constant reassurance to feel steady, you unlock a kind of freedom most people never taste. You become less reactive, more intentional, and deeply rooted in your own integrity. You're no longer swayed by every shift in your external world, because you've built a quiet certainty that lives inside you. And that certainty is not dependent on proof. It is built on presence.

Staying centered is also about developing your relationship with the unseen. When you cultivate inner stillness, you start to sense subtle forms of guidance that don't rely on tangible signs. A quiet reassurance in your chest. A gentle pull toward a choice. A deep breath that seems to soften your resistance. These small, often unremarkable experiences can be more reliable than the dramatic synchronicities we sometimes crave. The more you attune to them, the less you'll chase loud confirmations. You'll begin to trust the whisper instead of needing the shout.

There's a form of peace that arises when you stop needing the world to agree with you. It's not apathy, and it's not isolation. It's a grounded knowing that your path is yours, and it doesn't require external applause. That doesn't mean you shut others out or become closed to feedback. It simply means that your center is not up for negotiation. You carry it with you, quietly, without asking the world to validate it at every step.

Sometimes, the proof comes later. Much later. You may find that a choice you made in solitude years ago blossoms into something meaningful only when the time is right. It might not come in the form you expected, or it might not even look like success to others. But you'll know. You'll remember the moment you followed that silent knowing. And you'll recognize the unfolding not as random, but as aligned.

The most powerful transformation happens in the space between what is and what will be. This is the gap where no one is cheering you on, where the path looks foggy, where you have nothing to show for your effort yet. If you can stay rooted here—if you can continue to show up for your own truth even when no one sees it—you are becoming someone unshakeable.

It helps to stay in close contact with yourself. Notice what grounds you. Maybe it's a quiet walk. A few minutes with your hand over your heart. A conversation with someone who holds you without needing to fix you. These are not strategies to control the outcome. They are ways to come back to your inner authority, again and again. And in doing so, you train your nervous system to stay open, even in uncertainty.

You may still long for signs. That's human. But as you evolve, your relationship to signs will shift. You won't need them to believe you're on track. Instead, they'll become gentle echoes of what you already know. A reflection, not a requirement. You'll no longer read silence as rejection or the absence of progress as failure. You'll understand that inner alignment sometimes looks like stillness, and that's not only okay—it's sacred.

As you deepen this inner resilience, life starts to feel less like a test and more like a conversation. One where you are no longer desperately asking for evidence, but quietly listening for the next step. You stop waiting for permission to trust yourself. You stop needing things to prove themselves in order to believe in them. You begin to embody a steadiness that others can feel, even if they can't explain it.

There's a quiet kind of leadership in that. A presence that says: I know who I am, even when the world doesn't mirror it yet. I trust the timing, even if it's not mine to control. I walk this path, not because it's been confirmed by others, but because it's been confirmed by the stillness within me. That kind of presence doesn't need evidence. It is the evidence.

And when the world eventually catches up—when the signs arrive, when the outcomes emerge, when others begin to notice—it won't surprise you. You won't need their recognition to feel whole. Because you've already been living the truth, long before it had proof.

A Last Word: Thank You

If you've read this far, then you didn't just read — you traveled.

You listened, questioned, softened, and remembered.

You gave yourself time. You gave yourself trust. And that is no small thing.

There is no final secret, no perfect map, no single truth to hold.

Only this: you are already more connected than you know.

The signs are not outside you.

They live in your pulse, your longing, your moments of stillness.

Trust that you will know when to listen.

Trust that what you've forgotten will return.

And trust that none of this is random.

Thank you for walking this path.

May your days unfold like a conversation with the divine.

And may you never again feel lost in the silence.

www.ingramcontent.com/pod-product-compliance
Lightning Source LLC
Chambersburg PA
CBHW060356090426
42734CB00011B/2156